Edna!
God bless you
Thanks for
support Cousin
Bertha Carson

I Am Who I Am...
A Work In Progress

By
Bertha M. King

Graphic Services Co.
Benton Harbor, Michigan

I Am Who I Am...

A Work In Progress

By

Bertha M. King

———•———

© Copyright 2002, Bertha M. King

ISBN: 0964872102

Published by Graphic Services Co., Benton Harbor, Michigan

Dedication

This book is dedicated to my husband, Otis King, Sr., my children, Kimberly King-Hopkins and Tara B. King, my nine brothers and sisters; Willie L., Dorothy, Lillian, Jessie, James, Walter, Rosa, Sandra and Eliza and in memory of my mother, Maggie Lee Hatchett-Johnson; to my three stepchildren: Elaine, Otis Jr., and Darren. To my relatives and friends who have been there with my family as I battled life and death physical challenges in recent years–I say "thank you."

To the New Paradise Missionary Baptist Church family; to the many women who have provided inspiration for my messages over the years; to the leaders and preachers who have allowed me to speak, motivate, and do retreats and seminars for their membership; to the many individuals who have requested my books over the years. You helped to create my vision. Faith, prayer, and commitment are the keys to my survival and the completion of this book. Thank you all so much from the depth of my heart for believing in me. Without each of your unique talents and gifts, this victory would not be as rewarding. Remember that God knows how to bless those who love him, especially when we know whom we are and the source of our contentment.

I Am Who I Am... A Work in Progress!

Contents

Chapter 1   I Am Who I Am

1. A Growth Cycle of Faith & Energy
2. Show Me Some Love!
3. I Am A Full-figured Woman With A Heavenly Endownment!
4. God Will Do Anything That Concerns Me
5. From Fear to Faith...
8. Operator in the Prayer Room!
9. Life Is Only A Letter To and From the Savior!
10. If You Want Me to Make It – Criticize Me!

Chapter 2   You Can't Get your Blessing Until You Get the Lesson

12. God Did Not Bring Me This Far to Leave Me!
13. Tell Me About Trouble!
13. I Got Beat Up On My Way to My Blessing!
15. A Miracle is Happening...
16. Who in Heaven's Name Left the Gate Open?...
18. I Got What I Got and Nobody Can Take It Away!
19. Called to Preach, Teach & Reach in An Urban Wilderness...
20. A Leader of Substance in A Land of Plenty!
21. It's Our Time to Say "Amen"
22. Forgive Me Lord...
23. Thank You Lord!

Chapter 3   Culture Creates it's Own Stories of Survival

25. I've Got Roots!
26. I Am Free!
26. You Can Call Me Mama or Step-Mama–But You All Belong to Me!
28. Can I Have a Talk With You, My Brother?
29. Sitting in the Front Seat With a Back Seat Mentality!
31. How Do You Know That He is Your Man?
33. Freedom Begins With You!
34. Is the Man of the House At Home?
35. When You Are Black, Tell Me Where is Your Hope for the Future?
36. Why Martin Luther King, Jr. Day?

Chapter 4   Strong Women of Adversity in Times Like These

- 38. Standing on the Promises of God!
- 40. What Life Didn't Provide, Mother Had in the Love of Her Children!
- 44. How to Overcome the Odds & Make Positive Things Happen for You
- 46. Watch me!
- 47. Is Anything Too Hard for God?
- 48. My Premiums Are Paid Up: Where is My Policy?
- 49. Sh' Sh' Don't Tell Nobody...
- 50. You Know You've Got a Nerve!
- 51. Praying for Strength When Being a Woman Is Not Enough!
- 52. The Scars Come Out At Night...
- 53. Saying "Goodbye" Is a Choice!
- 54. This World is Not My Home, I'm Just Passing Through!
- 59. Tribute to a Pastor's Wife
- 60. Dialysis Is Not My Master, It is My Testimony!
- 61. Define Parenting and Reap the Benefits
- 63. Can These Bones Live Again?

Chapter 5   Winning the Battle While Wrestling With Spiritual Demons

- 64. I See Dead People in the Land of the Living
- 66. Faith When The Odds Are Against You!
- 66. I'm Crying–Who is Listening?
- 67. Halo of Depression
- 68. Eulogy of the Devil
- 70. I See A Light: Is That My Breakthrough?
- 71. Lord, I Give My Life To You!
- 71. I Am a Selfish Friend–Don't Leave Me Alone...
- 73. My Tongue Has a Sweet Savor
- 74. I Met Jesus At the Pool of Saloam!
- 75. Encouragement Is Like a Letter...
- 76. You've Been Down Too Long!
- 77. You Can Be a Christian and Talk About Love Between a Woman & A Man!
- 79. This Song Is Dedicated to the One I Love!

Chapter 6   Poetic Reflections of Love & Realities of Life

- 81. A Parent's Pride As Nature Salutes!
- 81. Every Day
- 82. See the Handwriting On the Wall!
- 82. Take a Look at Yourself
- 83. My Mother
- 83. Thank God for You, Mama!
- 84. Dear Church School Member

85. Our Power Is Always Nigh!
86. Don't Let the World Fool You!
87. What Can I Say?
88. Mama, Do You Hear Me?
89. Family Reunion Blues
90. Preacher: Access Your Members!
90. Who Wins in this Game of Love?
91. Who's Afraid of You?
92. I Weep for My People
93. A Child Born to Drug Addicts Can Be Saved!
94. I'm Not Tired Yet!
95. What Is Life Without a Friend?
95. To What Do I Owe This Honor?
96. Who Am I?
98. You Can Make It!
99. I've Only Got to Look Around Me!
100. A Lady but Still Mama's Baby
100. Kimberly and Tara: My Jewels

Chapter 7   There Is Humor In the Church As Well As Our Lives

101. I Stand Accused But Am I Really Guilty?
102. Ain't Church Funny...
103. Don't Fight the Heat Waves that Burn Inside of You!
106. What Happened to Us? When Did We Get Old?

Chapter 8   Life's Many Messages to Comfort & Guide Us Professionally

107. A Healthcare Professional On a Mission of Integrity & Faith!
108. People Perish for Lack of Knowledge & Commitment...
109. Survival Is Life's Make-over for the Soul!
111. You Are Not Defeated–Stand Up & Accept Your Success!
113. Life Is Like a Kitchen Singing the Diversity Blues!
114. You Can Play on God's Team If You Know Your Position

ABOUT THE AUTHOR

Bertha M. Carson King is a native of Benton Harbor, Michigan, and a nationally-known motivational speaker. King is the founder of Car-King & Associates, a consultant firm specializing in the areas of diversity issues, team building, management development, self-esteem, employee communications, teen workshops and empowerment sessions and parenting seminars. She has been published in the International Library of Poetry anthology *A River of Emotion*, and has written a play, lyrics to a song, and a recorded inspirational message. She is a frequent speaker at schools, colleges, conferences, workshops, seminars, and churches.

King is known as a woman of courage and conviction; a leader and a motivator; a source of strength and dedication; a teacher and a life-toucher; and a believer of God and the power of man. She is active in her church: she is a Bible teacher for the Junior Missionary Women, Sunday school instructor for the women's class, former scholarship chairperson and current member, and soup kitchen coordinator. King was also the first woman Kiwanis President in the Michiana area.

King's diversity and communication experiences range from education of adults and youth to issues of minority access to healthcare and diversity best practices. She has received numerous commendations for her down-to-earth approach to work ethics and conflict management resolutions. She has initiated several diversity projects which received recognition by local, state, and national representatives: The Memorial Hospital African American Leadership Initiative Group, The African American Health Professional Annual Dinner and Networking Group; and Access to Healthcare Project for Teen Moms.

King has over 30 years of employment experience in the private and public sector. She has received numerous service awards and she has numerous affiliations. She is a graduate of Western Michigan University, Kalamazoo, Michigan, with Bachelor's and Masters degrees in Communications, as well as secondary education certification.

Bertha King, who is currently recovering from a serious automobile accident and has a powerful testimony of faith "when the odds are against you," lives with her husband, Otis in Benton Harbor, Michigan. They are the parents of two adult daughters, Attorney Kimberly King-Hopkins of Tulsa, Oklahoma, and Tara King of Benton Harbor, Michigan. She has had to personally relate to change and goal setting.

Her philosophy in human services is, *"You are not responsible for what others do and say to you, but you are responsible for what you do and say to others."*

Chapter 1
I Am Who I Am

A Growth Cycle of Faith & Energy

How can I explain to those who do not know me that *I Am Who I Am*? I am complex and yet, I am so simple in my lifestyle and outlook on life, that most people take me for granted. Of course, once they get to know me and understand that my demeanor is by no means the sum total of Bertha in her euphoric-state of energy, they may make false assumptions. Rest assured, that "I Am Who I Am!"

I refuse to apologize for my womanhood, my ethnicity, my family, my age, my home, my status, my education, and any other tangible and intangible belongings that I enter a relationship with. For those who feel that they owe a debt to the powers that be for their livelihood, please feel free to pay in full your debt of gratitude, but my decision has already been made. I am looking forward to the day when I can reach beyond my past misfortunes of immaturity to a new day, a new beginning, to a new source of victory. A human source, perhaps, who wants to become a team member of diverse strength, ready to battle the elements of negativity and despondency accepted by the unmotivated of a dissatisfied world. Yes, there are reasons to be angry and justifiably so, but that is energy I cannot afford to waste. There must be people like myself who feel that we must run this race with fervor. Run as fast as we can, because the barriers are being erected and to ignore the urgency of time is to watch others collect the prize which we have worked so hard to attain.

We cannot be pessimistic about the future. Neither can we be so enamored with dreams of the future that we forget to assess what we bring to the table of strategic foresight. I am looking for miracles and cannot afford to only look up and down and fail to remember that there is a front and a back. When one side is covered and difficult to comprehend–always know that there is a way. It may not be your way but it is there for your convenience. I've learned to look for my miracles in out of the way places. Places that others don't see because they are in a "beauty" state of mind.

What is a "beauty" state of mind? It's a time in life when everything looks good and if it doesn't appeal to the eye, something must be wrong with it. People tend to walk around it and ignore it because to stop is to take something away from them. Can you believe that mentality exists? I beg to differ with you and challenge you with my own theory. I believe that one out of 10 people have similar opinions. Imagine, if you will, that a woman meets a man and he is homely as "homemade sin." Most women would not give him the time of day. Why? Because he is considered ugly. Many things are equated to him because of his looks. Let's personalize him more. He is a high school graduate, hard worker, clean, loves his parents, loves children, and wants to own a home. A "beauty" stage of mind won't see any of that. They see looks and what is. Enter the scenario: a good looking woman, praying for a meaningful relationship or maybe not, but she spots this man.

What man does she see? First of all, this woman is focused on, not the beauty, but the potential. The diamond in the rough. She has seen what they can have together! With some "loving management tools and some self-awareness techniques– this woman and this man will create a love machine which will create a successful marriage. Given the right ingredients and the resources, she has a college graduate, an industrious mate who believes in equality and bears no malice regarding her role in a male dominated society. As a queen of her home, she treats him like a king and the world is confused because they see only what they classify as Beauty and the Beast. They have not a clue that the Beast is in their eye sight and is to the woman like honey is to a bee. The beauty becomes secondary to a practical philosophy. And lest we forget, this is only one analogy.

Who are you? What is your goal in life beyond right now? The more you plan, the better the results. I am so tired of people complaining about their lack of whatever, promised to them by somebody. They are empowered to do so many things but they are angrily and impatiently waiting for someone else to get the opportunity for them and, listen to this: you are expected to bring the opportunity to them "because they deserve it." Can you believe that? I can. I've seen it happen time and time again. When will people learn? Hopefully, the millennium will either make us or break us. As for me, I'm going to keep looking for miracles because, I am who I am, which is the sum total of me.

Show Me Some Love!

Show me some love and put your heart into it. I look for sincere expressions and honesty in all of my personal encounters.

Tom Joyner of the nationally syndicated Tom Joyner Radio Morning Show often says "it's all about love" and it really is a true statement.

When the arguments end and the grief subside, recognize that you need some love. There are wounded spirits sitting down on privileges extended to them. They are waiting for love to show up and provide rescue service. There are physically and emotionally challenged individuals still lying at the pool of their despair, who don't know that they can be made whole by saying the words "I am healed."

There are economically poor, homeless adults and children who have not accessed the knowledge that they can have what they believe to be impossible through faith. Have you ever watched the face and behavior of individuals who appear to give up on life? My heart aches to show them that there is a better way– through a greater faith. I want so badly to say "you have not because you ask not."

Or better yet, say as Jesus directed, "Ask anything in my name and I will do it." When you have been poor so long, it is "mind-boggling" to believe that you can achieve even a measure of success. How do you explain to doubting people that a God who made everything–who owns everything–who creates all things can manifest every thought, every request and bring to pass all things?

There are drug-addicted, mentally challenged, cancer and diseased individuals crying out in their bondage to be saved from their ravaged conditions. If we were to stop and ask for their greatest healing prescription they would say "show me some love. Show me that you care. Show me that you have faith in me and in the power of God. Show me that you, my friend and confidant, are praying for my deliverance. I want to know the total cost of your love, in comparison to mine."

What is love to you and I? Love is greater than any substance I have yet to encounter. It looks beyond faults and finds the good. It searches beyond the surface to find the inner beauty which few will see unless they come near the recipient. It shoulders and smolders beneath and above the compassion and sometimes the passion of the giver without restraint and fear of the unknown.

Hurting and stressed individuals don't care about your degrees or college affiliations. They want to know whether you are down-to-earth and real in your associations. They want to hear you converse with enthusiasm and energy. Can you hear them share appreciation when you laugh and comprehend their dialogue and southern interpretations? They want to see a spiritual connection between you and I and the Heaven that we talk about. Their renewal will demonstrate to us a miracle sitting in the sunset of time.

I'm A Full-figured Woman With A Heavenly Endowment!

There is no shame in my name, my size or my eyes. Folks have to recognize that I am a prize to the one who realizes that my God, my heavenly father, chose me out of a field of many he created. For those who dwell on physical features and plus and minus–get a life and grow to be all that you can be. I am a satisfied, sanctified saint who happened to come wrapped up, tied up and tangled up in God's love. I've got more than the critics can begin to explain because my Father owns everything and then some.

If I ask him for the stars, all I have to do is wait for one to drop low so I can reach up and bring it down to me. If I request a promotion, I only have to believe that the job is mine. I need a husband and if I ask him to select one for me, I know that he will do what is best for me. When I dream of success and prosperity, God will make it all a reality and call it a "blessing."

Size is abundance in my book and I wear mine well. What I brag about in my testimony is my heavenly endowment. You see Jesus paid for it and I am a recipient. What you see is not necessarily what you get because there is more to me than meets the eye. I walk tall and carry a love stick. I love because I have a Savior who first loved me. My love stick protects my self-esteem. It also encourages me during some of my troubled days. I used to get upset at "fat" jokes and negative comments but I learned how to move beyond things that appear to block my progress. This is my body and my persona is aligned with my identity. As long as I know who I am and whose I am–I am somebody.

There is no secret to my magic which works for me every time I ask for a miracle. I asked one day for a financial blessing (I pay tithes and offerings). God opened his windows of Heaven and poured me out a blessing too numerous to count. Then from all directions the blessings came, running over, pressed down and shaken together. You have to see it happen to understand why I cannot be sophisticated when I shout and praise the Lord. I plan to leave something intrinsic as well as extrinsic for my family and friends when I must leave this journey. It must be something that will last long after the tangible things are gone. It will remind them of faith and strength, of perseverance and beauty in the soul of one so gracious.

I am not intimidated by small women, no matter how they look. Why you ask? The answer is that I do not have to wait to be affirmed by others and their standards. I have a great big Daddy, and a loving Brother, who is as "bad" as he wants to be. They are usually busy and dealing with one crisis or another, but they left the greatest "Baby-sitter" of all time–the Holy Spirit. When others are mean and vindictive to me, my "Baby-sitter" who is a comforter and friend, speaks soft words of peace to me. He continually provides me with gifts beyond my imagination which abundantly bless my spirit. I am full-figured, proud of it and so richly-endowed.

God Will Do Anything That Concerns Me

There are days when I feel that I am not making it. Times when the weight of the world is on my shoulders and I want to throw in the towel. Times when the pain of rejection and hardships over the years try to conquer my soul and I have to remember that the price has already been paid. Crying seems to be obsolete because it appears that my tears have ceased to flow from the fountain of my despair.

I have to remind myself that there are no rewards for those who start and stop on this life highway of trials. The voice of reason and consciousness tells me to remain calm, for my help is on the way. It reminds me that this is not the first time I will go through storms and it won't be the last. It comforts me by reflecting on the victories of the past and promises for my future. Oh, but it is difficult to move beyond what I am feeling right now. I want to blame somebody for my challenges and there is no one visible but me. There is song in the Negro spirituals that shares a message of hope and truth with me when I want to blame a person or circumstance for my misfortune. It says "Search me, search me Lord, and if you find anything that should not be, take it out and strengthen me, because I want to be saved– I've got to be whole."

Listen, if you can begin with yourself, half of the battle is already won. When my problems are compounded and fears regarding their impact are pressing me on every side, I literally stop my blessings from multiplying. Why do I do that on the eve of my victory? I'll tell you why! The old me–the insecure, unregenerated me–interferes in the process by reminding me of the past failures and the uncertainties of the future. It puts my focus on those who don't like me, who criticize and mistreat me. That ugly, deceitful, lying, miserable side of me comes to take the beauty from my spirit. It wants to see me crawling and fumbling rather than calling and humbling myself before the almighty God who gives good gifts. This part of me does not celebrate my opportunities but it rejoices in my inequities of yesterday.

However, there is a word, a revelation from the only one who can make a difference for all concerned. King David in Psalms said that God would "perfect all that concerns me." I believe in my heart that there is truth in that passage of scripture for I have used it to declare freedom for my children and my home during moments of turmoil. When we pray and ask for peace, love, deliverance, joy and stability–why not believe that our faith in God will work everything out for the best. I'm standing on the promises, on the word, on the strength of a living Savior who promised never to leave us or forsake us. Therefore, when I am at my extreme or so it may seem, that is the time to let go and let God. If I am in God and He is in me, I am told to ask and He will do what is required. That allows me to know that He is perfecting (taking care of what I asked) what concerns me (what keeps me up at night, what causes me to shed tears, what distresses me) and I trust Him because He can do it better than me.

From Fear to Faith...

When was it that I first felt my pain increase? How did a car accident that left me untouched outwardly create such havoc within me? How could I have worked long hours and with stressful situations without knowing the ultimate strain and injury to my physical person? Why didn't my physicians and therapists treating me on a regular basis check the test results and physical abilities to determine my health needs?

As you can probably surmise, I have a lot of questions but few answers. What I have learned in the process is more about me and my faith. I have discovered that I am lacking in areas of my spiritual beliefs and feel increasing discomfort in the knowledge that I, who teach and advise others, need a refuge for my soul. Ten months ago, I was in a three-car accident, of which I was the victim. My car was totaled and I was told that I probably had soft tissue injury. My immediate thoughts were that I did not need medical attention and that I would go home and recuperate from the obvious pain. As a matter of fact, I heard just the opposite. My doctor sent me to an orthopedic physician, who sent me to outpatient therapy, who recommended additional options, none of which indicated the seriousness of my health.

My physician went on pregnancy leave and I found myself needing assistance on a day when the pain was unbearable. Therapy was not available because they had canceled my appointment because I am only eligible, by doctor's orders to see them once every three weeks. At this point I started to feel less secure about my health and contacted a chiropractor in my hometown. He readily agreed to see me but refused to treat me when he saw my condition and MRI as well as his own x-rays. He also requested that I allow him to send my results to Kalamazoo, Michigan to an excellent neurosurgeon, Dr. Harris Russo. To make a long story short, I was asked to meet with him and the diagnosis was not good. My condition had advanced to a life-threatening condition and there were concerns for paralysis. I was shocked to hear the information presented to my husband and me. I was advised to meet with another physician, a spinal orthopedic specialist, also in the Kalamazoo area. A week later I met with Dr. Bruce Dall and was devastated at the end of his discussion with my husband and me. It seemed that they would have to do extensive surgery to help me.

Dr. Dall's plan, as was Dr. Russo's, was that my neck, front and back, would be cut for extensive fusion of my neck discs. A bone in my left leg as well as one from my pelvic area would need to be removed to be used in the rebuilding of my neck. The results would be an improvement but I would have a neck that would not bend, in all likelihood. Talk about heavy-duty realization! I was devastated. My world as I knew it was fading into some imagery which I could not fathom. I hurt now as much within as I constantly did on the outside. I kept thinking "God, what is he saying to me?" Why is this happening to me?" What have I done to deserve this punishment?" Then I reasoned briefly within myself and thought "He is evidently talking about someone else and I'll wake up and this will all be over." But of course, it was I, standing in the need of prayer. It was not my sister, not my brother, but me, oh Lord, standing in the need of prayer.

On the way home, I cried softly as my husband drove and the pain was so intense that I felt the depth of my despair. I listened to my gospel music that brought such comfort but there was none that day for me. All I felt was "what will I do?" To make a decision to do this was unbearable because I had plans developed nationally and locally that would mean so much for my future. And here, I was on the threshold of my victory, crying in my midnight of storms. I could see the noon skies and hear the busy flow of traffic but to me, this was a midnight of pain beyond an accident or anything that I had physically experienced before. I felt violated at the prospect of being struck down while minding my own business, even angry and frustrated at this turn of events. I would have to stop working at a job which gives me so much satisfaction in each achievement to benefit the organization and public we serve. Now I was being told to stop driving and stop working because everything physical was now a problem for me.

For two days I gave in to self-pity, refusing to eat much of anything. Slowly I began to receive the Word of God through prayer, scripture, and television evangelism. Friends hearing of my dilemma began to call and encourage me through love and prayer. My strength was mobilized through seeking for the Lord's assurance that everything would be all right. I started praising God without restraint and putting my focus in asking for a miracle to take place. As I prayed I looked beyond the pain and the decision required to a heavenly solution that very well might result in surgery. I now had the resource and strength to get up and make it through the storm.

My story became a supplication unmatched in my storm-filled life. I began to talk to God with a fervent belief of His intervention and healing of my emotional as well as physical body. He was present and we needed to make a spiritual connection without interruption. My request went something like this: "Lord, I'm standing in the need of prayer. I don't know where to go or who to go to but to you. I am weak but thou art strong. Help me to feel your spirit in my weakness. I need a doctor and a friend. The doctors are wonderful but you are the Master Physician. They tell me that it is not good and my life will change but I'm asking you to let me be a testimony of faith. Nothing is too hard for you. These doctors don't really know me and I don't know them–but you made all of us. You gave them the knowledge to deal with the sick, help them to find that miracle moment for me. You can do it because you have done it before–over and over and over again.

You can fix this body because it belongs to you. You made it and you put every bone where you knew it would operate efficiently. I am your child and I'm turning this body over to you right now, with all of its imperfections. Help me to be better, Lord. I know that you did not bring me out of that car to leave me. You did not keep me safe for ten months without a plan. You did not allow my doctor to be on maternity leave and the other physicians to step in on time without a plan. On that premise I believe that I have the faith and You, my Lord and Savior, have the power to let this miracle take place for those I have been witnessing to for so many years.

You told me that I could ask anything in your name and you would do it. I am asking without fear and without hatred toward any person. Years ago, you anointed me to be a light among your people. I am taking the torch and making preparation to sit on a hill of this distressed city, waiting to lift up your name. I thank you for allowing me to "look to the hills from whence cometh my help." I love you so much because out of all that I have been through, you still love me better than anyone else."

In the midnight hour, I received a revelation to look in the book of Genesis for consolation. I was reminded of God's creation of man and how He performed the first supernatural surgery of the universe and breathed into man the breath of life so that he would live. I had insight into the birth of a woman through the process of a rib being surgically removed from the side of the created man and she received the breath of life in order to be made whole. My Holy Spirit was trying to tell me to "be still and know that God is supreme." I was comforted in the knowledge that "with God all things are possible." Nothing is too hard for God. When the doctors, with all of their skills and abilities, give their diagnosis, faith in the Master Physician will bring the miracle healing and cause them to know that they are limited but He is not.

I don't know what tomorrow will bring, but I know who holds the future for me. Today is my future and my hope is built on nothing less than Jesus' blood and His righteousness. There is peace in knowing that nothing can come against us that God will allow to harm us. I see the problem, I hear the solution and I know the source of my contentment. The world must know through this ordeal that joy and peace comes from a risen Savior who heals and delivers in an appointed time.

I believe that prayer and the Word of God will see me through. His Word is medicine to our healing and we must look to Him. Friends look at me and shake their heads when I tell them that I am trusting in God for my deliverance and healing. I am an overcomer on my way to victorious living. What they cannot comprehend was before too high for me to reach but in my hour of need I have truly met my Savior. He talks with me when I feel the least of all and whispers in my sleepless nights that I am not alone. I know now, more than ever before, that "the Lord is my Shepherd" and I don't have to want.

My life has been a testimony but never like this. Never have I felt the presence of the Lord Jesus resting in my spirit like this. I think it is because we claim faith and profess belief in Jesus but it is at the throne of mercy and grace that we really find the cross. From this moment, songs will never be the same for the message will have a greater meaning. Sermons preached with fervor and reverence will never be the same for I am hungry to gain greater privileges through the Word of God. People through me will know Him because if He can do it for me, a Benton Harbor welfare child, they will believe that He will do it for them. The Master is working with me and I am growing in a time when I am expected to give up in defeat. I have given up my fear–for faith and power in a living Savior who tells me that I can be healed in spite of the medical predictions and prescriptions. As a child of the King, I can "walk through the valley of the shadow of death and fear no evil for God is with me." I want you to understand ahead of time that there is victory in the name of Jesus. If we can't ask God for a blessing, If we can't ask for a miracle–for a breakthrough, for a friend, for love, for hope–tell me, who can we turn to?

Operator In The Prayer Room!

Where do I begin? I remember sharing with you my movement from fear to faith as the physicians prepared me for surgery. (See story on Fear to Faith). I was so concerned about the need for immediacy with my surgery that I failed to recognize the hand of God in delaying the scheduling of my procedures. I could not understand why the same physicians who advised me to quickly make a decision were now telling me to wait. Here it is in September and they want me to wait until November. If I am as critical as they both said, then someone should be making plans to get me in to the hospital. After all, look how long I had already suffered.

The week of my surgery arrived and I met with the physician on Tuesday; surgery was scheduled for Thursday morning. When my husband and I were shown to the appropriate room, I began to pray. I asked the Holy Spirit to let me feel His presence. To know that this physical journey was making a turn beyond my control needed greater assurances than I possessed. I could feel a presence, warm and comforting, that enveloped the room and I knew that God was in my corner. The doctor came in and began to look through his notes. He seldom smiled, perhaps because my case had little to smile about. Quietly, he explained that he had had time to review my MRI results and felt that he could avoid taking the large bone from my leg as planned. He wanted to use a plate and screws instead but felt that these would be safe and successful. Remember my concern for the delay and yet, the delay is what gave the doctor time to review my case. "Thank you God for your amazing grace. You are always on time."

I cannot describe my joy and the peace that surpasses human understanding. My doctor was looking at me strangely because he still had to go in the front of my neck, the back of my neck, and the pelvic area and I was thanking him for the words he had shared. I had asked the Holy Spirit to intervene in this invasive operation which was scheduled for eight hours. As the doctor was leaving, I asked him if he believed in prayer. Whew, when he said he did, the room got brighter. I requested prayer and he volunteered to pray. The three of us held hands and prayed. Without consciously thinking about what I was saying, I told the doctor that God was not through intervening in my surgery. While I was speaking, thoughts of the doctor thinking me crazy kept surfacing but I could not stop. I thanked him for the news he gave me and told him that I was expecting a miracle. He smiled and told me that we would keep praying. When we left his office, my spirit was so uplifted for the first time after leaving a medical building since the news of my condition.

Time will not allow me to give all of the details leading up to my surgery but I went in on Thursday with faith that the Trinity would bring all things together for my benefit. I looked around at my family as they stood by my bed and I knew that God would bring me through. When I woke up in the recovery room, I learned what prayer will do. My family was so jubilant and shared with me the good news–the doctor did not operate on the back of my neck. He was able to do the procedure through the front of my neck and remove the bone needed from my pelvis. I wanted to shout but the body said "no." My surgery was not eight hours but five hours.

The next day Dr. Russo, my neurosurgeon, arrived first and he shook his head as he told me how close I was to being dead or a quadriplegic. He felt that everything had gone well with my surgery. We had to wait and see. I will always be grateful for his efforts to help me and for his referral to Dr. Dall, my orthopedic surgeon.

Dr. Dall finally came and I could not wait to share with him my thanks for hearing God's request for me. No one will ever know what answered prayer means to those who have nowhere else to go. He sat down by my bed and I said my thanks. Before he left, he whispered "God told me what to do." Earlier I had shared with Dr. Dall that I was going to write him a letter regarding what God wanted him to do for me. You talk about being a privileged child of the King! I was ready to minister to anybody who would listen but my family kept saying "don't talk or move too much." Little did they know that this sister was a believer and now an achiever.

Instead of four to five days in the hospital, I was sent home in two days. I was so angry for being "thrown out" of the hospital in my condition. But listen, what I forgot was my miraculous healing, request to God. The medical staff assured me that I was doing wonderful, my vital signs were good and my procedure was in order. I did not feel wonderful. I was in pain and on Morphine. I could not see that the blessing was already in place. Everything that was amazing to the others was just right and on-time for God. What a mighty God we serve.

Life Is Only A Letter To and From The Savior!

Dear ____(Name)_____:
I am an observer of life, seeking a refuge for my soul. I know about your good works for the Lord and because of the Lord and because of the love your friends and family have for you, I wanted to share these words with you.

I write these letters in your behalf. Have the best day that you can on your special day because life is but a letter to and from the Savior. A blessing from God that has been stamped "Return to Sender, delivered as anticipated."

_____(Name)_____, if you were to write a letter addressed to the Lord, I believe this is no doubt what you would say:

Dear Master,
Thank you for hearing my cry throughout the days of my life. Thank you for patience when I thought prayer was too slow to move my mountains. Thank you Lord for wisdom like Ruth in waiting on your special blessing. Somehow I don't feel no ways tired 'cause I've come too far from where I started from. Lord, nobody told me that the road would be easy but I can't stop now 'cause I've come too far from where I started from. Heartaches, pain, sorrow, disappointments, tears, and loneliness come to all of us. Sometimes I have felt that I have endured my share and some of others as well. Then I remember Romans 8:28 when it says, "And we know that all things work together for good to them that love God." Ephesians, the 5th chapter taught me what I need to wear when I start on my journey fighting Satan and his Army of unbelievers. You brought me up as a child in your word. You were the potter, and I the clay. Together we have traveled time. I've had to be molded, broken, rebuilt, and pressed in order to develop and receive your holy spirit. Master,

in sealing my letter, I want you to sign me up for the Christian Jubilee. Please write my name on your roll. I've been changed since your love lifted me. I shall be ready when you come.

Your Servant in Christ,

If You Want Me to Make It–Criticize Me!

I get so tired of "mess." Day in and day out–mess from those who pretend to care about your welfare. Folks, you know well and those you presume that want you to make it. You want to believe their rhetoric and then they shoot you dead in your self-esteem. There isn't any justice, or rhyme or reason to their methodology.

In spite of the negative forces that come against us we have to find positive means of fighting adversity. I cannot speak for others but I have coined my own phrase for survival in a "dirty world." It is built on this premise: "If you want me to make it–criticize me. Tear me down and press me so hard with your jealousy and hatred that I cry without understanding why. Destroy my name and discuss my lack of social grace and watch me hold up my head in gain rather than shame. Look always for the darkness of my past and ignore the light that has conquered the shadows. And better yet, keep smiling in my face like the perpetrator you are and fail to see the true friendship that smiled back at you with no reservation."

I want to stop with my regards to you, whoever and wherever you may be, but I can't stop now because I have kept it bottled up too long. You see, I thought you would have mercy and quit after a while but you persist and I can't resist telling you about my victory. "Oh yeah, I cannot count the times that I saw you and our mutual friends laughing at me and I pretended that I did not see you. Saving face in the presence of so-called friends was everything to me at that time. You all told me how proud you were of me and my accomplishments and then threw cold water of sarcasm at the distance I traveled to get to this point in my life.

What folks don't understand is that pride envelops my spirit when I think of how my family overcame the hardships and heartaches of the past. What we did not have–we did not miss–because when you have little, you tend to be satisfied with little. When you learn better, you tend to do better. Being poor ended up being a blessing for me because I learned to appreciate abundance and scarcity.

You think you hurt me every time you told a lie on me but every lie helped me to get to the truth. At first, I thought I had to prove myself to others in the face of the lies but I learned that silence can be golden at the right time and the right place. A lie will only support you for so long and then it leaves you sitting in the witness stand waiting for a witness to bail you out. You never knew the tears and the fears you all caused me. Time has a way of healing wounded spirits and broken hearts and some of us are mighty grateful.

Family folks, friends and church members too, wear the adversarial badge of criticism. Folks you thought would support you and then you learn the hard way that everybody is not in your corner. There were times I thought I was losing my mind and was discontented at my lot in life. There were times when my physical body was in pain and the doctors shared news that was not good. And there you were to let me know that you were there for me. You reminded me "that what might have been done in the dark was coming to light." You spoke to me in past tense and questioned whether I had talked to my family about my condition. Except for the grace of God, I would have given up or taken a bus to visit relatives who would have really taken me there. (Everybody who has been there in concept will know what I mean.) I have come to a conclusion and there is a joy within and without that the devil in hell cannot put out. I have experienced the grace of God who gives understanding and privileges above and beyond what man is able or willing to give. He has anointed me to inherit what you did not reveal. He is willing to give me what you have concealed. He has promised me that He will give me more and more and more, running over, pressed down and pouring out of the windows of heaven that I cannot receive it all. So laugh and mock and point and insult, but know this out of all you know: No one can touch this!

You don't know who you are messing with. My Daddy and my big Brother are sitting on a gold mine up in a place called heaven. A place where there are no lights because diamonds and pearls light the way. The streets up there are paved with gold and I can walk them any time I get ready. The good news is better–I don't have to die to receive His blessings. I can ask for anything and my Daddy will give it to me. I can ask my Brother who loved me so much that He was willing to sacrifice His life on the cross for me. He died for you too but you were adopted and didn't get your papers signed and that's why you don't know that you are messing with a relative. Check the record–it is all in the Bible–our family history. So when you talk about me, you are talking about yourself. That's why I never answer when you come to me talking that negative "yang talk" that is none of my business but affects my investment.

Now if you want trouble: Keep bothering me and watch and see who will come to my rescue. All I will say is: These are my relatives. They are worse than any gang. You may be afraid of the street thugs but they have nothing on the Heavenly Club. I warn you not to make them angry because they do not play. You may not see them when they come–but you always know when they leave–that they were there. I don't have to call you names or talk about you. I don't have to put voodoo powder down at your door. There is no need for retribution. All I have to do is love you and my case is already made. How do you like me now?"

Talk is cheap unless you can back it up and I am backing this thing up with the word. The scripture says that a man will reap what he sows. Psalms 46:10 says that we are to "be still and know that He is God." John 14:14 says "Ask for anything in my name and I will do it." What can I say? I say "time out for mess, never mind the rest. All that happens to us is a faith test and if we stand, we are blessed. Come on criticize me some more. I can take it or fake it 'til I make it. If you want me to make it in this life–criticize me and watch it happen right before your eyes and you can believe me or not–that is a natural-born fact!

Chapter 2

You Can't Get Your Blessing Until You Get the Lesson

God Did Not Bring Me This Far to Leave Me!

"Why me? Why do problems appear to find me in my weakest moments? What have I ever done to make folks treat me less than the best? Do I deserve to be criticized and rejected by those who have known me all of my life? What right do they have to judge me? Questions invade my peace of mind in order to block my goals and achievements. I try to rationalize what might have occurred in our interactions to cause the animosity and negativity. There are some possible foundations in a few cases as I think back over the years, but for the most part, a foundation has not been laid. I cannot understand or comprehend what has set this psychological process in motion.

I do know that I want to get off this whirlwind of theories and suppositions regarding what is happening.

Eventually, paranoia creeps into my homogenous mind and I become suspicious of everyone and their motives. There are few people that I choose to trust and many to accuse. It is easy to become a recluse and stay out of enemy territory. I see issues in every gesture, every word, every look and every action. There is failure in everyone but me according to my philosophy, and I refuse to change.

One day I find myself falling victim to my own assumptions and suicidal tendencies become a refuge rather than something horrible and self-defeating. I know that I must get help or I will be overtaken with no hope for deliverance. But when I reach out for help there is no support system because I failed to include them in my rush to judgement. No one, it is clear, stands ready to speak up for me in my moment of distress. Names fail to surface as I search through the recesses of my mind, the phone directory and faces from networking that are projected in my memory but not necessarily pleasant to recall. What is a woman of fear to do? Must I continue to suffer defeat after defeat? Must I be the one to cry and shoulder all of the blame for my condition? What about the ones who treated me so badly? Why should they go unscathed as I deal with the aftermath of low self-esteem?

It is while the questions and innuendoes are coming that I realize that I have been my own worst enemy. Here I am at my age with no lasting relationships, no family to speak of, little money, a house that is not a home, and few loved ones to communicate with. This is a "deep revelation." I am not sure that I am ready to deal with the significance of my reflections. As I decide my course of action, I begin to feel as though I am in a box which is self-imposed. It has limited my potential and caused me to imprison my goals, my heart, my physical presence, my mind, and my soul. I have made a huge discovery: My soul is not for sale and I had pawned it to justify my selfishness.

Where did I go wrong? When did this madness begin? How did I allow these feelings to affect wonderful years of my life? Time has become an ally and there must be a way to overcome what has been a devastating situation. In my moment of greatest frustration and hopelessness–I called God. I dialed 1-1-1 through prayer and implored my Master to forgive me and allow me another opportunity to know and appreciate His will for my life. I know without hesitation that God heard me and answered my prayer.

I am stepping out on faith with a renewed determination to make a change in my life. It does not matter who is for me or against me because I have an understanding of my past. I have crossed the time zones of indecision and acknowledge that human beings are limited in their ability to control other individuals. In my pursuit of justice and freedom for the rights of others, I have released myself from my own locked-up successes and abundant choices. When the keys began to open the final doors of the dark recesses of my mind, I knew joy that I never thought possible. I am humbled at the knowledge that has been available to me all these years. There is a quickening to my spirit and a lift to my soul when I think about the peace that I have found.

If you were to see me today, you would marvel at the woman I have become. I live to smile and to engage with others who smile in return. It is not important that they give me a kind word as we greet each other, but it is important for me to look for words of welcome to give to them. What a blessing to be able to have peace of mind on the best day of the rest of your life.

Tell Me About Trouble!

Every time I seem to be making a way and getting ahead with my life, trouble comes to stand and mock my progress. "I'm going to fight back this time," I say to myself and then retreat with tears and frustration as the heat treatment begins.

One more time and I'm going to give up and die because every round is higher and more painful than the time before. And you know what? The next event causes me to lie because I am not in control of what happens to me. It is at this point that a distinct message hits home. This world is not my home and I own nothing that can prevent me from greeting trouble over and over again. There is no power that I possess that can turn life-threatening situations around unless it is driven by my esteem choices and faith in God.

There are folks obviously counting my misfortunes as though they have a stake in the process and that is their prerogative. However, they don't know nor do they understand, that I have an advocate who loves me more than I could ever describe. He knows how much I can bear and how blessed I am. Those who stand around looking for a reason to tear me down or interfere with my praise should recognize that I am God's child, protected from all harm and danger. For those who love me, I have coined a phrase: "Don't count the times that you see me go down–count the times that you see me get up!" By doing so, we both learn to trust the prophetic word of God who promised never to leave or forsake us.

I Got Beat Up On My Way to My Blessing!

If I had the wings of a dove I would fly away like David said in Psalm 55. I would take my heavy load, drop it in the sea of time and sail away to be at rest.

When you are an over-comer, your life experiences are vastly different than the average Christian citizen who cannot understand your stress and tears. There are survival tips and suggestions for those who are going through a series of trials and are not sure if they can make it. Let me share with you some expectations and give you some encouragement.

I battled a life threatening illness and God brought me through the storm of suffering. I learned that everyone is not happy about your victorious testimony. Your so-called friends and well-meaning relatives will find ways to discourage your good days and encourage your sad days.

Even your job organization will put demands on you in terms of benefits and insurance that you find hard to believe. When they discover in your absence, the many positive roles you play, they may put pressure on you to return. This is after knowing that you are medically unable to perform at maximum level. Do not see this as happening only to you. It happens to most people who are visible and valuable in the employment sector. Ignore your desire to walk away, when you know you need the benefits. Do what you have to do, legally and morally, and continue to heal. No one can harm you in this game of life unless you allow yourself to be defeated.

People may call to see how you are doing and you wait to hear the inevitable "when are you coming back to work? It's been a while and you seem to be better." Mind you, these are the same individuals who saw you suffer while you worked and felt that you were a fool to come to work in a obviously painful condition. I know about being "beat up" in the work place but I also know about getting up to get my blessings.

Your insurance providers may have sent you numerous letters about your value as a customer but watch the climate change when you submit a claim. If you are a long-term health or injury claimant, you will know the difference. Pay careful attention also to the dynamics of your insurance premiums as they define your "care package."

I have been amazed and stressed out literally for expecting my insurances to benefit my illness and recovery. Every week brought a new revelation, often several days in a row. "Beat up" was not a frame of reference initially, however I have adopted this phrase after recent attempts to have bills and benefits paid. My first thought was to throw up my hands in defeat. The Holy Spirit admonished me to throw my hands up, say a prayer and to remind myself of my yet unseen blessing which is coming.

Maybe you haven't been beat up on this walk of life. Maybe your dreams have become a reality without the drama and violence attached to it like so many others experienced. Maybe you have not had family members reject you for growing educationally and emotionally. These are the times when you learn to smile at the malicious references and speak up with love and peace as negative behaviors approach you.

Getting beat up physically does not feel good or look good. A "good" fight leaves scars within and without. If you can acknowledge that you've been beat up – there is hope. If you will admit that you are hurting–faith in God will be a refuge and a healer. When you recognize that circumstances cannot take possession of your soul, your spirit will rise to the occasion.

I am starting to expect a miracle in spite of what comes against me. It is not easy to endure a war when you appear to be the victim. The victory is in knowing that Satan can only do to you what God allows him to do. He thinks he knows me but God knows me best. My father in heaven has assured me that "greater is he that is within me than he who is in the world."

The apostle Paul also gives me encouragement when he writes "I can do all things through Christ who strengthens me." I must remember that the battle is not mine, it is the Lord's. I am tired of being beat up but if the fight means that I will be blessed beyond the hurt, beyond the sorrow, beyond the persecution, beyond the humiliation–then I will assume the position.

A Miracle Is Happening...

May I tell you about my dream? No, not Martin's dream. It's my dream and I know that it will be a reality. I've been up and down so many times that I have to remind myself that a better day is coming. No one can see the possibilities like I can when I share my story. Folks think I don't see the smiles and the heads shaking when I turn my back but I know what I know. I know what faith can do and that is my purpose in talking to you.

You are walking around with your head hanging down, believing the worst about your situation. Yes, I am talking to you! You look and act just like I used to when I felt defeated. Have you forgotten who woke you up this morning? Have you failed to remember Genesis, Chapter One when God made everything and it was good. He made your man too, and you know he's good to you? Think about what He created and who He made and then think about the problems you think are insurmountable. Honey, we serve a risen Savior who got up and shook off misery and agony to give you and I a reason to live. Get up from there and get your miracle. God promised it to us on Calvary and reminded us from birth that we would be a part of a heavenly kingdom. Don't you tell me that you can't make it when your grandmama and my grandmama had nothing, and yet they professed everything when they worshiped a living Savior.

Don't you dare come in my presence holding out your hand with a needle or a pill in it, trying to tell me that "you ain't got nobody." I wish you would come in my face and tell me about folks lying on you and scandalizing your name but that you have faith in a living God. Woman, you better think about corn bread and beans with water for supper and maybe rice with a little sugar over it for the next day. Perhaps you can recite with joy your daily prayer for the "daily bread" you've been given. Look for your miracle in out-of-the-way places. Places where common folks, doubting folks, never think to look. If you are going to give up, do it boldly for a reason. Do it after you have tested God's word.

I know this does not make much sense to you, but in order to live as a whole person you have to have a source of help. You need a refuge when dark days come to destroy your confidence. It is easy to talk "mess" when things are not going as you planned. You can still have victory because you are willing to defy the odds against you. Too many things have come against you which tell you to avoid a negative stand. Hold up your head and smile at the adversary. He knows your stamina but he does not know your battle plan nor your limitations. Only you can allow the adversary access to the source of your contentment.

I believe we can do what others do not suspect. We are destined for greatness and I know we are too close to give up now. Get up and let us be about our Father's business.

Who In Heaven's Name Left the Gate Open?...

Who in Heaven's name left the gate open to blessings untold? Who left the gate of opportunity and prosperity open for those who are considered outcasts and despicable residents of a decadent society? Tell me who determined the process for entrance into the Kingdom of God?

I don't know who left the gate of Heaven open but I am glad that a wretch like me was able to access the premises. I would hate to be arrested for breaking and entering God's house when He so graciously accepted my invitation to come into my life. As a matter of fact, you cannot enter God's Kingdom without a key, purchased and examined by the Master. A key that was made from the blood of Jesus and established by the Master Locksmith. There is no power on earth that can make another key from this model which has numbers etched on its front: 1-1-1, representing the Father, Son and the Holy Ghost. Without all three in operation, the door will not open.

There are methods to learning the doorkeeper's identity. We who are students of the Word have to know our source of power and deliverance. Let's look at several means of entrance through the gate of Heaven:

• Self-Esteem – the self worth of a person; their abilities and capabilities; the way they see themselves in the scheme of everything else.

When you feel good about yourself regardless of your condition and circumstances, there is hope for a better today and a greater tomorrow. What other individuals say about you becomes less important than what you say about yourself. You begin to look for ways to enhance your knowledge, your self-respect, your attitude and your plan for success. When others betray you, for whatever reason, you tend to think about promises beyond what the world can do to you. You begin to talk the talk of gospel proclamations "No weapon formed against me shall prosper." Folk will marvel at your humble spirit while acknowledging to others that "you are not one to mess with because of God's love for you."

• Faith – the substance of things hoped for, the evidence of things unseen.

Think about it! If I can see the object, the goal, the thing that I desire, why do I need faith? It is already available to me for the taking or the asking. What effort is required to obtain it? If the answer is none, then the question is non-existent. My blessing is through the Word of God, standing on the premise of a zero balance working things out for my good. At the same time, there is no evidence of success and no witness of victory. My word, respected though it may be, has little bearing on what I profess to others as faith in its purest form.

What the critics don't know is that I have friends in high places who look out for me on the orders of the Most High God. When I try to explain my faith in a Sovereign King who owns everything below, around and above, I see sympathetic looks and uncomfortable silence. In the wake of my testimony to family and friends, I see and hear what they are not saying and that is okay too. After all, I was once in their position of not having a foundation of faith which sees beyond the impossible mountains and suffering "maybe's."

In the midst of the uncertain moments and the tests of time, I see a glimmer of hope begin to surface in the darkness of my mind, designed to reclaim the Word of hope. I begin to move with confidence among my enemies and so-called friends. I lean not to my own understanding but to God who sees all and knows all concerning me. There is a door ajar in the distance and I tell myself that if I can just make it in–I can still have a refuge for my soul. I can still have joy and prosperity that surpasses human understanding. I see a miracle coming through the open door and now I know that faith in God can do anything but fail. I have His indwelling spirit and together we are awesome.

- Passion –That burning desire to act on a decision, to love that person, something or a commitment to a goal so much that you will do anything legally and morally to make it happen. You can feel it, taste it, see it, and be it, in the vision that you have regarding your achievement.

What you want will happen because you are motivated and your faith in God will substantiate it. Don't apologize to anyone for your behavior and attitude that loves your dream. You can do anything with the powers at your disposal. You have blessings beyond belief in Heaven's Storehouse and without passion for His Word you cannot attain them. The door to the Storehouse has limitations and is open only to those who have invested in the business. The hours are flexible and the customer service is extraordinary. Those who visit do not always depend on sunny days and pleasant afternoons, but they often visit at midnight and in stormy weather. There are no special sales and the prices are wonderful to all who care to come.

What is that you say? How can you get a membership card? Did I hear you say "who do I need to know to get an invitation and when do the doors open?" Your membership is in coming to Christ, acknowledging the Lord as your Savior, confessing your sins, and baptism by water. There is no one except Jesus who can get you into the door of Heaven. There is no other way to enter. He has a standing invitation: "Knock and the door will open. Seek and you will find." The Word of God also encourages us to look for blessings. According to the Apostle Paul, "We have not because we ask not."

There are so many opportunities to prepare for miracles and blessings promised by the Word of God. Jesus Christ left the door open for you and I. He knew then that we were imperfect and fickle creatures of habit and yet, He chose us to enjoy His gifts of life and leisure. We are loved in spite of our sinful minds and spirits that lead away from the throne of grace. Through our suffering and trials in this life, He has promised never to leave or forsake us. We must thank Him with every fiber of our being for what He has done for us.

The door was left open and the Storehouse is available. I won't steal or kill for my portion because it is too much for one lifetime. What I will do is leave the door open for you through my blessing if you choose to enter. Otherwise, there is more than enough to go around individually and collectively. You don't see what I see and I cannot possibly see what you see, but I know what I know and who I learned it from. Hold out your hands and walk through the door of God's promises because He did not, would not, have left the door open for me without a reserve key for you who have also come up the rough side of the mountain. Who left the door of Heaven's gate open? Read the Word and live the life and you will know your purpose and the reason for divine transformation of those who come into the presence of God.

I Got What I Got and Nobody Can Take It Away!

My mind has been transformed and renewed by the power of the Holy Spirit. There is more to me than you know or ever will see. He has put all good things in my path and told me that they belong to me. You don't have to curse me, hate me, or block my way because I operate under God's orders and my steps are by design.

I have become hungry for the Living Word which fills me when I seek for truth. I am blessed when those that I love and trust betray me and refuse to have anything to do with me. I am learning about me more and more as I study the Word. I now know that some of what has happened in my life has come because of my unfaithfulness and impatience. I am responsible for decreasing my own blessings and blaming others in the process. One example was the strong desire to get a credit card. Five thousand dollars later–guess who was crying? You got that right! It was me standing in the need of a Savior, money, and forgiveness.

I am a pleasant individual who was brought up to know right from wrong. I want to please and be pleased but if not, oh well. A self-made woman, a visionary, propped up with truth and energy derived from hard times, I exude motivation. I have determined that I will make it. Survival with my back against the wall is not new to me. You have to be there at that point in life, when enough is enough and your spirit refuses to be broken. A time when you know you have crossed that line of demarcation and cannot go back. As a matter of choice, you don't want to go back.

Some folks got their knowledge from a school book or heard a story while sitting around a campfire but I learned first hand from ghetto crooks and inner city, southern wisdom cooks. As my grandmother, my aunts and my own mother prepared a meal, they taught profound lessons through conversation. As girls, we were primed for womanhood and admonished about young boys and deceitful old men. I got what I got from those who had their own "homegrown experiences." They paid a price for every privilege and because of them, I enjoy greater opportunities. Those women whom I remember with love today gave me more than the college professors could research on a good day. They schooled me about money and I now keep a "piece of money" put away privately for heaven knows what may come. I will never forget or downplay the messages I received in those days. Most of them are gone now and there is an empty place that must be continually refilled from my storehouse of knowledge. My family and friends benefit from the indwelling spirit that guides me to greater understanding of those who are a part of my life.

The essence of a woman's heart is directed by God and I thank Him for what He has done for me. The world's standard will not dictate my success or failure because my prosperity and abundance begins with my own tongue. I got what I got and no one can take it away. No one can take what Jehovah God has ordained and proclaimed as my inheritance. A merry heart according to the proverbs has a continual feast and so do I when I got what I got.

Called to Preach, Teach, and Reach in An Urban Wilderness…

When God called you to preach, teach, and reach in an urban wilderness, I pray that you were inspired and guided by the Holy Spirit. We are in a spiritual warfare with our adversary, the devil. He comes to steal, kill and destroy. The only power he recognizes and fears is the almighty God and the name of Jesus Christ, the Savior of this world. He is not afraid of you and I unless we profess the power of God and live accordingly. It is up to us to remember that we are children of the King.

We are enemies of the satanic forces of the devil. Our goodness–he meditates. Our love–he hates. Our loyalty–he exaggerates. Our services–he tries to regulate. Our hope–he negates. Our faith–he shakes. Our peace–he separates. Our downfall–he celebrates. This master of evil operates in the wilderness of our mind, in the haven of communities and walks in the cloak of darkness. He cannot be trusted in the morning of our harvest. He may talk like us but the anointed man and woman of God will discern the true character.

In the essence of your heart, there is a testimony waiting to be shared because of your wilderness experience. I remember crying several years ago that "I had been through enough and couldn't take any more suffering." I had marital problems, my house burned down, my mother was dying, my first-born left for college which was out-of-state, and my car overturned with my husband, my 16 year old, and myself. My personal testimony became stronger because I learned to lean on the strength of God. He alone could soothe the pain and hurt too deep to utter. What was too much for me was just enough for God.

For those of you going to battle with the enemy, you need to understand the enemy that you are fighting. Learn to research the enemy camp and how to escape if you are discovered. Only a fool would walk into enemy territory, waving a dish cloth and singing the blues. I have a few suggestions for you if you plan to fight the battle of your life:

• Have a battle plan that is built on the truth and has the input of a team of qualified veterans who are knowledgeable of the adversary's tactics.

• Dress for victory with the assurance that you are protected.

• Expect to win, for losers will perish without a vision. If you can't see it–it ain't happening.

• In an urban wilderness, be prepared for street ministries. Don't assume that because you announce "I am a Christian" that people will rush to embrace you and believe that you are sincere. If you serve the Lord with gladness, God will sustain you so that you consistently teach the Word. "To whom much is given, much is required" the Holy Bible reads, therefore, you get up and meet the challenges of the mission before you.

• Above all that you do, pray without ceasing. You do not have the strength to stay mentally, physically, psychologically, and emotionally equipped to fight Satan. Without prayer, you will lose.

Did you think that you would announce your calling and run to an organized pulpit in order to draw the wilderness folks into your ministry? Did you assume that the demons of alcohol, drugs, diseases, sexual sins, hatred, racism, gambling, and other infirmities would cease to exist when you became a preacher or teacher in the urban wilderness? The response would obviously be "no" because there is no paradise here on earth. There is no utopia where needs of the poor don't press forward to grasp for a scrap of bread, a message of hope, and a small degree of comfort. This world is not our home, we are pilgrims passing through. The people you serve think this is their home and that you will provide for them–that you are a voice crying in the wilderness of their despair.

You are tired before the battle begins but you cannot stop. You cannot give up because the enemy has declared war on you. You cannot see the adversarial forces coming against you because they work beneath the surface to undermine you. Some of them (spirits) are in your own camp and you don't recognize them, although Christ will expose them in due time.

You have got to be ready to move when the Holy Spirit tells you to move. One promise to keep close to you during your service is that God will not put on you more than you are able to bear. When we receive our calling–God provides for us. When you think your life is unbearable, there is assurance that the Lord loves us more than anyone will know. We must learn to be careful and content despite the situations we find ourselves in. We do not necessarily have to like what is happening but when we consider the choice we have made, just remember the joy that cometh through the hearts of men as souls are saved.

We are blessed in our urban wilderness experiences. We have an advocate for lonely times and endless battles. All we have to do is ask for God's presence when we need consolation. Our joy, my brothers and sisters, comes from asking and receiving blessings that only a Father can give. You may have started in the wilderness but with a few good workers and our Savior, you can clear the area and build a city of worship.

A Leader of Substance in A Land of Plenty!

Show me a leader who comes from the ranks of the impoverished and I'll show you a motivated leader with a group of dedicated followers. A leader of substance who came from the outhouse of the past to regurgitate after a thorough cleansing of their sins has unlimited power. They have been anointed with a calling on their lives that few can deny.

Show me a leader who knows how to smile, and I'll show you a leader who draws individuals like fishermen. Fishermen who consistently draw fish into their nets of service and abundantly reap the harvest. Show me a leader who is compassionate and I'll show you one who receives bountiful blessings from God and their membership. A leader who communicates, in addition to the other virtues, is in high demand. Trust and loyalty are crowning glories to add to a glowing biography.

Is there such a person who will approach the roster with enthusiasm for the success they have garnered in their groups? Is there a leader who stands outside of the church house who is a power house of prayer and a stronghold of faith? Can you show us one who serves gladly without a mandate or bylaw to determine whether they are active or not? Can we find one who can withstand the temptations of the adversary and look to the hills where all of their help is derived for their blessing? I want you to know that there is an Advocate for those who meet the criteria of a Christian. There is supreme evidence to support that one does indeed meet the criteria required. The Holy Spirit will direct you to the source of your salvation.

A leader who refuses to sell out will be marketable for years to come. Quitting is not an option when leadership is a priority. When a firm "no or yes" is necessary, a strong leader of substance will emerge. Popularity must not be a motivator unless the leader understands that when the party ends, so do the accolades.

Even though things may be going well for a God-sent leader, he or she must not forget the poor in a time of poverty, although it may be physical or mental poverty, as they stand at the well of their despair. These individuals need to hear from a servant leader, an overcomer, one who may have seen a mountain and through prayer was able to make it over.

Integrity will bring triumph if you are willing to maintain a sense of dignity and respect. There will always be opposition, but a leader of substance will rise above the suspicion and criticism, to achieve their breakthrough. People may not like them but they will respect what they bring to a situation. It may seem that the organization is going under until the leader recognizes the power that one person possesses that can affect change. One person, with a purpose, strengthened with passion, and unique abilities, can turn a negative into a positive. This person can restore hope and vitality into what was once thought to be a "lost cause."

A leader of substance can mobilize a storefront into a picturesque ocean view. They may be driving an old jalopy, now known as a "hoopty," and then you see them buying a luxury car. Their hand is seen in regenerating a miserable, uncommitted group of individuals into believers who become prosperous and faithful. Many who before were non-Christians will begin to seek for spiritual guidance. No true leader ought to speak publicly of only their accomplishments but praise the entire group success. It will gain them respect and honor from the membership as well as favor with God. The more that the leader receives, the more they will be entrusted with.

A leader of substance who looks for opportunities to give rather than to receive will stand tall in the community and the church family. Blessings will overtake them when they least expect a Word from Heaven. The poverty mind will disappear as the leader chosen by God is elevated to peace and joy that only a Father can give.

Who is this individual of whom you speak? It is our servant leader of substance in a land of plenty!

It's Our Time To Say "Amen"

If you have been hurt and abused in this battle called life and survival, this is your time to say "amen." It is your time to hold up the flag of surrender, not in defeat but to the glory of God. After all, this battle is not yours–it is the Lord's.

You cannot win by yourself. There is no power in you to fight a spiritual war alone. Without God's help, you are up a creek without a paddle. We both remember our past and the bondage we have had to overcome. We are miracles standing in the presence of a resurrected Savior. The world knows only a part of our history and what they know may not be accurate. You and I are conquerors for we fought a hard fight in order to see this victorious moment. It is time for us to put our mistakes, our faults and failures behind us and move forward. When you have been broken and the potter has put you back together again, you have to witness regarding his goodness. Our purpose is greater than filling a pew in the sanctuary and singing "Amazing Grace." We have been set free to free others from ignorance and discouragement.

It is our time to sing hymns of joy when tradition requires quiet and solemnity. With what we have overcome, there is no need to apologize for our prayers, our shout of acclamation or our smiling countenance. Our bills have been paid through trials and tribulation. The devil in hell cannot reap the benefits of our suffering. It is our time, yours and mine, to say "Amen" and to wear our victory with praise and Thanksgiving. We derived our rewards from the spoils of the wicked. This is our time to rejoice and our hearts have predicted that the time is "right now."

Forgive Me Lord...

Lord, please forgive me for the sin I have committed in my life. Forgive me for waiting too many years to give my life to you completely. I played while others prayed and then I stayed in the juke joint (the bars) and clubs for much too long. I learned how to cheat and became a professional gambler at life's game of chance.

I wanted to be accepted and I attracted the unacceptable, disrespectful people who cared little about anyone but themselves. New clothing and a few dollars was my primary objective and I frequently purchased them. I wanted men, not one man, but men in the plural and you would assume that I picked them from the horror pages or comic strips. I laughed when I should have cried and cried when I could have laughed. God's Words and His blessings have always been available to me but my spirit was not always of God. If I knew then what I know now, I never would have chosen the life I selected. I know that I cannot blame others for my choices and situations. I had fun, or so I thought, until I had to pay the cost for the wrong I did. It was I who generated much of the suffering and hardship I experienced.

When we are going through a "season," we tend to remember whether it is "sin oriented." In areas of our life such as spiritual, financial, physical, psychological, and social, there is a correlation of divine retribution and reaping that everyone goes through. This is not to say that everyone who suffers has done wrong, but there are some of us who have been richly blessed in spite of our negative choices.

We have done enough to tear down ourselves and God's kingdom. It is a wonder that we are still standing in an upright position. And don't mention the church actors and actresses who refuse to change because they discovered a playground in the sanctuary. From the pulpit to the pew, we have designed our own set of rules rather than the ten commandments.

We have learned to justify our sins without regard to the damage to God's kingdom and the lives we exemplify. This is my fervent prayer: "Forgive me Lord for my part in these deceptions and give me and others another chance to be healed of our transgressions. We've needed a physician and the medicine was accessible but we did not take it. I am ready to be offered up and set free from bondage and destruction. Please do not turn away from me. Bring me through this mess in my life, Lord, for I need to be delivered. I am afraid without you by my side. Touch me so that I can be blessed forever. I want to testify even to those who know my sins, because they need to recognize a cleansed soul who was lost but now is found. Thank you Lord, for saving me when I lost my self respect and the peace that used to come naturally."

It took a miracle for me to admit to myself that I was wrong and needed a Savior to heal me. If we who are saved are to make a difference among God's people, trusting the Master is a prerequisite to the journey. We must ask for his forgiveness and mean it from our heart. He can and will answer prayer. Talk to him and it does not matter whether you are sitting down, standing up, lying down, or looking up–it's all good because He is not hard of hearing.

Thank You Lord!

I woke up this morning and viewed the cloudy sky with despair. Burdened and disillusioned, I counted myself the least of all. My life seemed so dark, hopeless and dreary. I began to think about the surrounding forces and their meanings to me. I thought of the blind who will never see the sun shine and somehow my day seemed to brighten. I fell to my knees and gave thanks to the Lord for all He has done for me.

I said, "Lord, Thank you for the morning and the clouds, for it was in darkness that I first saw the light. Thank you for the blind. They know the secret of 'Yea though I walk through the valley of the shadow of death.' They've stood on the deck of the old ship of Zion and heard about the thousands who have landed. Lord, help me to know their joy and to stop complaining."

I had no job and felt sorry for myself. Everything in my life caused me concern. My bills were piling up and my table was often bare. I wanted to give up when I heard about a man named Jesus and a substance called faith. I sought for knowledge about the Savior and found a refuge for my soul. Someone sang a hymn one day entitled "If the Lord don't help me I can't stand the Storm," and the answer returned "The Lord is my shepherd and I shall not want. He leadeth me beside the Still waters."

I've got little materially but I am rich because my Father in heaven has my inheritance. He has promised to give me the desires of my heart, and all I have to do is ask anything in His name. He said that He would supply all my needs according to His riches in glory. I'm standing on His word and holding on for His miracles. Love is my mission and righteousness is my basis. I can do all things through Christ Jesus who strengthens me.

There was a lady sitting alone by the side of the road believing that her life was not worth living. She sat there, in despair, contemplating how to end her life. Her complaints were many but her noticeable handicaps were a missing arm and leg. I shed tears when I heard her cry "Lord, why me? What have I done to suffer like this? I can't bear these afflictions!" Standing over to the side of her was a man, shaking badly, who could not stand because he had a severe disease. He moaned,

"Master, help me to be strong. This pain is more than you can imagine. I don't believe you lifted me out of sin to leave me in this condition." I know Jesus was standing in only God knows where, saying "My children remember the crucifixion. Remember the love I have for you. Love so strong that I gave my son, in suffering and shame, for people who mocked my name. I know your sorrows and your hurts. Wait on me and I will strengthen your hearts."

While the man and woman both sat there, draped in sorrow over their losses, a heart-wrenching groan and words of misery were uttered from still another woman nearby. She said, "Oh God, why have you taken my family from me in that terrible fire? My husband, my children and all I possess are gone. Why now, when we had everything to live for, and we valued each day, each burden and problem? You kept us through our sins and fed us when we were hungry. I don't believe folks love you who are doing all kinds of evil and still you've let them live. I can't understand it! The wounds are too deep. Help me to know the answers." She began to sob uncontrollably.

Not one of us spoke a word nor made a sound, but we listened and wept for this woman's loss. Amazed, we heard the woman quietly speak again to God, with a quiet and remorseful tone. "Forgive me Father for questioning your wisdom. You are the maker and the creator of all things. You owe me nothing. Not my life, my husband, my children or my home. All that I am–I owe it all to you. The abundant peace you've given to me and even the trials that set me free. I cry because the flesh is weak and the agony of death pierces my soul. I must go on with my living testimony because somebody may be praying for encouragement and the only one to help them will be your witnesses who have overcome this world. Your blessed strength and peace will help me to make it."

The woman looked over at the rest of us and smiled through her tears. I never shall forget her remarks to us. "The Lord owes us nothing. Jesus paid it all on Calvary. Whatever you want to do in life, know that you have a Savior who carries His grace, packaged for our needs. If you love people, show them while they live, in ways that matter, for tomorrow is not promised to you. If they reject you, love them anyway. Some people we learn to love from a distance of respect and mercy because they are troubled and wounded. They want to hurt and insult but we are protected by the Holy Spirit. Nothing can harm us that God has not tempered with grace. The enemy cannot stop love. In spite of our conditions, we've got life and with life comes hope. We've got to get up from here and look for miracles and opportunities to give thanks for what we have. We can't bring back yesterday because if I had the power I would do it for all of us.

"Other people will not understand us and our tears. They don't know how to calm our fears. Only Jesus can mend broken hearts and repair battered bodies. Let's take the time we have right now and expect the impossible from that which is possible.

"Thank God, for we are only a few of the chosen ones wearing our badge of courage. Look around you and see others who are facing even greater trials than you and I and have learned to endure. Yes, you've been put down, talked about, walked on, and perplexed. You've been denied love, but get up and have a beautiful day, for it is one that the Lord has made."

Chapter 3

Culture Creates it's Own Stories of Survival

I've Got Roots!

"Every tub has to sit on its own bottom. If you make your bed hard–lay in it. Tend to your business and I will tend to mine. Sister, you had better watch your mouth or your behind will give you a check that your butt can't cash." My grandmother and mother would say all of this and more on a regular basis. The quotes that I've given are only a few of their profound tidbits regarding urban life.

Interesting enough, the media and the majority have termed inner city living as urban but the economically depressed minority call it the "ghetto," "Country," "the hood," or "danger zone." No matter what the label, to many it is considered "home." Many of its residents are connected in some way, by crime, poverty, workforce alliances, intimate relationships–legal and illegal, children, churches, education and politics. I have always marveled at how news travels faster than the speed of light without the aid of eye witnesses, phone calls, computer, binoculars, flag raising or smoke signals. I'm not saying that technology is not being used–but that people will find a way of communicating events without any assistance. They will relate details as though they were on the scene. Mind you, that the newspaper and radio versions will likely differ from the resident reporters. They always have the "inside scoop" straight from the horse's mouth. Unfortunately they will not reveal their source because it was told to them in strictest confidence.

These are representatives of my history. Folks who know who my daddy is or who my real "daddy" is–if I allow them to whisper in my ear. I have to smile or laugh outright because some of my own elder family members, in the south and the north, believe that Clark Kent, alias Superman, is real and lived in Saint Louis. Don't ask them, please don't, to tell you how they know, because it is a long and mind-boggling story. On the other hand, there are those who can see everything in a dream about somebody else, but can't see Johnny Ray, their old man (boy friend) courting the next door neighbor.

I've got roots and was never allowed to forget them. The cultural way of talking, the charisma of loving those I care about, my smile that reaches beyond the pain remind me of who I am. The work ethics instilled by my parents and grandparents remind me of the cotton fields, sugar cane, and tobacco plantations somewhere in the southern, hot labor lands of this great USA. My soul is embodied with everlasting peace and praise for what I am able to give back to others coming behind me.

My roots will allow me to with stand the degradation of the "lingering stigma of racism," a subtle reminder of the class systems within a culture, and the inept efforts by some to second-guess my intellectual abilities in a professional decision. My roots dictate that I must not give up. I can't give in to the belief of inadequacies others want so badly to label me with. I must always remember that I exemplify a tree, rooted and grounded in a firm foundation. No one can put me down without my permission and I refuse that challenge any day, any time, and to anybody. You see, I am a living reality of a dream that one day I will be judged by my character and not by the color of my skin. A reality that one day I will not have to search for ways to ignore the ache in my heart when someone is served ahead of me. I have a dream that I will be able to go to the bank and withdraw any amount that I desire without being in debt. I want to be able to tell my friends and foes that I have found peace in spite of my circumstances. My dream is similar to Martin Luther King's dream but his dream is not my dream. I want to be loved and appreciated for what I bring to a relationship and to celebrate the knowledge that "it's all good."

We need to recognize that roots are important in family life. Another expression that I heard often was "the leaf don't fall too far from the tree." That statement was made when someone would exhibit behavior or attitudes similar to their parents, elders, or older siblings. My mother and grandmother are gone now and I miss them more than I can say. The humor of what they thought and others like them will always be my reason for survival. When I think of all they endured, with few advocates to speak for them, determination becomes my guide and faith my protector. I am a woman borne of hardship and blessed with substance. Bessie Smith sang a powerful song in her day– "Mama may have and Papa may have but God bless the child that's got her own." I am proud to say that "with my background and a testimony to boot–I got roots."

I Am Free!

Thank you Lord for setting my spirit free from jealousy and envy. Thank you for allowing me to see beyond material and physical things to a knowledge much greater–the spiritual power of God. A power that demands respect and obedience. One that rewards me by providing the resources necessary to my survival as well as those I request for my pleasure.

Since I learned what my freedom means, I accept nothing less than the best. Bondage cost me my self-esteem, peace of mind, respect and my integrity. I cannot afford to have time rob me of the precious gift of making the best of what could have been a sad situation. The power of self-talk is not new to me but in order to grow into the person I want to become, I have to pray at all times.

When I confess my desires, my inadequacies and expectations, I am releasing my faith. My faith then, embraces my testimony and delivers my blessings. I must stay in the Word of God so that I will realize that what was promised has been fulfilled. I am free to make things happen in my life on time and in time.

I am free to capture my thoughts and focus on tomorrow in all of its splendor. I am not talking about light years away but so immediate that you may not be through requesting with your mouth what God delivers at your feet. Things will change when prayer takes you to the cross and you are set free. Thank God almighty, that I have learned to be free at last.

You Can Call Me Mama Or Step-Mama–But You All Belong To Me!

"Come here, child. Come to your mama. Never mind the fact that you are an adult. What is important is that you are mine. Come here and put your head on my lap. Let me give you my nurturing touch of love as only a mama can do. You don't have to have a reason to stop by the house to get a hug–to feel some love, just know you can do it. I promise to listen and support you as you plan. You see I love you more than words can ever say.

Two of you came through my birth canal in a suffering way and three of you came over the highway and byways but all of you belong to me. When I said "I do," it implied a commitment to accept a ready-made family and I went beyond the limits most step-parents envision. I grew to love your uncertain smile and cautious hugs as you learned our immediate family behaviors and expectations. As newcomers, you tested the rules and regulatory codes of the household while your father and I demonstrated our parent leadership roles. We made sure that you understood the right-to-life policies and procedures as our two children recognized on a daily basis. Needless to say, you responded well to our love and appreciation, albeit slow for some. We shall not call names in order to protect those who now say they are innocent of all suspicious behavior while growing up.

We did not play the "tell my mama or my daddy on you" game either. You learned that we "mamas and daddy's" communicated with each other as well as with you. Your dad and I were respected and the feeling was mutual. I remember telling you–my stepchildren–not to allow my two children to pick on you or hit you, even though you all were older. After all, some small children are miniature "terrorists" with mom and dad's permission because they are so innocent and cute.

I pray for all of you more now than I did when you were young. Drugs and alcohol invaded our privacy and I am sad and angry at this intrusion. The enemy found some weak links and he worked overtime to destroy beautiful blessings that are so valuable to us. You each have abundant talent that make us so very proud of you. One day we will be victorious at eliminating the power of Satan from our family legacy. Prayers are going up and God is reaching down to take your hand in this journey of life.

To my own daughters who actually helped me give birth to myself through their love and acceptance toward others, I can only say "Thank you for allowing me to share my time and love." Through their self-esteem and my spiritual renewal, we have come so far to get to these times of dedication and restoration. As I gazed upon their vanilla and chocolate beauty as babies, my pride knew no limits. Today the reflection is no less and if anything, it is greater. God has been more than abundant with his love. I know that his grace is sufficient for me.

When I look at them, I see their father's resilience and determination to make things work. I see his features and habits that some times drive me to laughter or frustration. At times I see my smile and ability to support the less fortunate souls who need a friend. I see my temper when I believe I have done my best and no one seems to care. Two different individuals responsible for five distinct personalities, parts of us rolled into one. They are the ingredients that make us whole and complete.

Frankly, I don't appreciate the term "stepchildren." To me, it implies a "step away from the whole." We are family and that knowledge comes from a greater force within–that of Agape love. We could come together and play the imaginary game of "we tried to get along," like some families do while jealousy and envy permeate the relationship. We, however, prefer to have the real thing and that comes from the heart. With truth and faith in the spirit of family unity, love will keep us together for we are a force to be reckoned with. Where in this world can you find one person with so many qualities, from so many people? I bet I can show you some examples. They may have different names, a variety of birth places, a number of life experiences–but a wealth of stories about our special family history. We are not ashamed of how we came to be who we are. Our message is framed and presented in a broader context that may be of assistance for families who are struggling to blend when the mixer is not turned on.

Can I Have a Talk With You, My Brother?

Talk to me, my brother. How can you mistreat the woman who loves you more than anyone in the world? How can you abuse the best thing that ever entered your presence as a man? How dare you raise your hand to the twin rib of your body and the bones of your flesh? And you have the audacity to say in your moment of passion, when she has two black eyes and tears running like a broken faucet, "Baby, what do you have for your man? Don't be afraid–come to me and let me show you how much you are loved. Forget what the people say and remember that I am here for you." Call me nosy or whatever you choose, that is up to you but I say, "How dare you fix your mouth in a positive gesture after a negative self-esteem withdrawal. How dare you!

Talk to me, my brother, for I want to know how you can break the rules of love in the first degree. I want to know how you can hate those you love and love that which you hate. How can you go from friend to friend and discuss your disrespect for the woman God placed at your side but you cannot tell your woman how you feel? Don't you comprehend that her life is intertwined with yours and her blessings are a blessing to you?

I see the jealousy and envy when others approach you with joy at knowing your mate. I heard you downplay her role in the marriage, though it is obvious to all who know you, that she is your strength. You hide your financial gifts, that God's grace provides, not understanding that "God giveth and God taketh away." You don't have a clue that a woman was created as a helpmate for man. She was created to love as well as cherish him.

He was made to bless God and God gave him a woman to love and appreciate so that man would not be alone. God provided all of the intimate "relational equipment" to take the relationship to the next level of commitment. Do not ignore what should be a celebration because that woman, that chiseled work of beautiful flesh, is a part of you. What you do to her is a reflection of your own body and spirit.

Your children ought to recognize love at it's best because mama and daddy "got it going on." It would be a privilege for them to see their father kissing their mother as though he really cares rather than a perfunctory lip gesture. I don't mean an x-rated version but the kind of affection that translated means "this is my woman and I want the world to know it." Your sons ought to look for a woman "who exemplifies love the way his mother loves his father," and so should the daughter want a husband who, "cares like her father cares for the mother." I do not mean in a physical sense but in a spiritual and symbolic way that Christ meant. In other words, live the life that you talk about. Stop bragging to your friends about what a good relationship you have and then hide your mate from them after the assault. Talk to me, my brother.

My brother, I see you running to get to church in order to praise God, however, your family is anxious to see the man before them reflect the same enthusiasm at home. Although you are a great speaker and can sing like an angel, your tone and conversation at home is often critical and demeaning. When you get up, your wife and children begin to fidget and look at each other with unbelief. They wonder who the man is that lives through the week and the man of the Sabbath. Others see you as the epitomy of salvation and honor because that is the person they know and respect. They don't know you as your family and I do but time will bring the cycle around for retribution and you will reap what you sow. Talk to me, my brother.

Unfortunately, I cannot intervene without exposing my knowledge of family secrets. You really think Heaven is your lateral move to the top but I have news for you. You cannot get your break through without your mate. God gave you a blessed woman and you had better help her develop her testimony. He gave you anointed children and the seeds you planted early on will one day be ready for harvest. You are in need of a physician because you are sick and don't know that you need healing. It is not too late. You can change and rewrite the script of your life story. What you decide to do may very well set the record straight for so many lives.

Your father did not show love to your mother but you can change the cycle. You were hungry and now you can eat what you choose–what a bread maker we serve. You were nasty and dirty as a child–but look at you now, adorned in the best. You had no money–but the wealth of the wicked is laid up for you. Now you can ask for what you want. You were sick but it was God who told you to "get up and live"–He is a doctor in the sickroom. You were hated and God prepared a table for you in the midst of the enemy–God can do anything. He is awesome. His hand has been in everything that you required and desired to make a difference in your life. Don't take your mate through the hurts of your past so that she loses her way to her healing. Whatever comes to you must pass through you for her good so that both of you are bountifully blessed.

My brother, are you listening to my plea? Talk to me. You must get the Word of God into your spirit. You have a second chance to make the apprehension and frowns become triumphant praise of love and peace wherever you are. Forgiveness is the solution and change is the process–now, brother, let us pray!

Sitting in the Front Seat With a Back Seat Mentality!

These are difficult times to survive in. Your forefathers would probably have a different story regarding the hardships that we face in this new millennium. I cannot speak for them but I will for you. My hope for you spans an entire lifetime. I wish for you blessings beyond compare. My hope is for your deliverance when trouble attempts to steal your joy. My hope is for you to recognize love and capture the essence in your heart. My love for you is unconditional and makes no demand on your self esteem. I want you to enjoy the best of what life has to offer.

My concern is that you continually sit in the front seat without a "back seat-mentality." You have been more than blessed with perseverance to withstand the fiery darts of the enemy. The demonic forces of evil fly express from the depth of hell to defeat your dreams and plans for a successful future. They know that God has an anointing on your life. When you are trying to make it, there will always be someone waiting to pull you down. You ought to make it anyway.

In the south, where overt physical and psychological slavery existed, your ancestors were not allowed any of the privileges enjoyed by our white brothers and sisters. Don't get angry–get the facts from historical research projects. Through hardships and trials, they were unable to go to available restrooms and other facilities as others were permitted. Many educational opportunities were lost to blacks, prior to and during the civil war era, because they were not sanctioned by Jim Crow law. When the law was enacted, African American students were still unable to attend schools due to segregation and farm labor demands.

Any public gatherings were suspect and banned when the master felt that a group was developing something that might endanger the status quo. Employment choices were stereotypical and minimal when designated. Hotels and other public facilities were segregated. Any interracial relationship was a reason for lynching black males along with other murderous acts, even if it was consensual. Poverty was rampant in a land of plenty.

Why am I sharing this with you when things appear to be wonderful? I want you to know without a doubt that God's grace has no boundaries that you cannot conquer. You have a substance called faith that sustains you when your strength wants to give up. Take my advice, you won't regret it. Don't get back in the back seat of degradation that our forefathers fought so hard to survive in. I have watched you, on the eve of your victory, struggle not to go there emotionally. You cannot allow the pain of separation, when you have had disagreements, to block your ability to speak, or socialize with your sisters and brothers. Time is too precious for us to lose. You cannot afford to walk around depressed and angry because someone did not smile, shake our hand or tell us how wonderful we are. You cannot wait for the doors of opportunity to open for us–try making some doors for yourself. Remember, above all, that faith is working for you. When you realize that, you can ask for what you want because you know that all God has belongs to us.

You desire a husband or wife–don't sit back and expect a Denzel Washington or a Halle Berry to walk up to your front door and ask for you specifically. Get up and pray for guidance in your search and don't beat prayer by heading to the bar or to the street corner to find them. Wait and see if God will open up the windows of heaven and pour you out a blessing that you won't be able to receive at one time.

Just imagine that you ask God for a mate and one day, you look up and there he is. He has a limp. He has bad teeth and no physical appeal to speak of. He needs help from some source but you do not see it coming from you. This is not your dream come true. But when he gives you a smile and shares with you his goals–you can see potential, with God's mercy and grace. You begin to see the power of the Holy Ghost at work in this relationship. Years later, you can witness to all who will listen, that you love this man that God gave to you. The good-looking man with the limp, nicely dressed, beautiful teeth, hardworking, dedicated loving man, father and husband, who has your back.

Trusting God will heal the wounds of time and soothe the hurts that so often bring about tears. Many people have been delivered from the bondage of drugs and alcohol, sexual sins, gambling, abusive relationships, lying, and stress, to name a few. God gets individuals out of one situation after another and they find a way to put the chains back on.

Education is accessible to those who will accept the conditions, study habits and sacrifices but some of us run past the school hall and find a pool hall. Some individuals love to stand on corners not understanding that many of our ancestors were sold on corner lots. We have the audacity to "sell rocks" to those who pass by us by while forgetting that we should be standing on the "solid rock called Jesus Christ." I want to say to my brothers and sisters on the corner that they are not in bondage. "Stop the madness and drop the rock that you are selling in order to invest in a sure return on your investment. You don't have to go to the street corner, in other words, the back seat of life, for your prosperity. You can come proudly to the front seat, public awareness of your skills and abilities, and take your seat.

Remove the frown and put a smile on your face while you move swiftly down the aisle to your source of contentment. Prosperity and abundance are sending you smoke signals to let you know that the time is now. When you have been attacked, cleanse your system with tears, put a band aid on–then get up and make it." My hope will be realized when you rise up and wave to me from the height of your dream come true. The front seat is where you find deliverance. The front seat is where you affirm that you have come this far by faith. It is the front seat that our ancestors fought so hard for you to sit in. And my child, it will be the front seat that you move from in order to make room for another sister who must leave the back seat mentality–just like you were able to do.

How Do You Know That He is Your Man?

Can you believe it? People can say things that will disturb your mind. Sometimes women, foolish women, will mesmerize you with tales of their relationships. I have to focus on one in particular, without a name, who will take you to the edge of reality. Let me give you excerpts of our conversation regarding her "man" and my observations.

"I got me a good man. I'm not afraid to tell it anywhere I go." How many times have we heard that expression and lo and behold there is a man in the love connection made on the shady side of town? The one who has the man's heart is a question for the psychic hot line. "What kind of mess is this?" I ask and nobody wants to be the first to speak for this is beyond revelation–a fatal attraction. And to top it off, she's got the nerve to tell folks that God gave her this man, this day, this chance, and this blessing from heaven. According to her it was all because she prayed for him and God answered her prayers. She intimated that she met him in prison but that was all right because he was accused unjustly. She also understands his deepest needs better that his wife ever did. They have complete honesty. No one can help him become a model citizen and loving husband better than she can.

Listen closely: She is going to take him to church for his salvation. The phone charges as well as others that he has accumulated will be paid by her in order for him to get a new start in life. After all, he deserved her help because most of the phone calls were made when he was so lonely for her while he was incarcerated. You know how it is when a man is depressed. All of her credit cards are up to the limit–he has to wear the best for job interviews. He has agreed to baby-sit her children while she works so that she saves on day care fees. There is no need to take the children out into the cold when she goes to work. He is even willing to take her to work and keep the car so that she does not have to worry about parking. Of course, he will be there to pick her up after work. These thoughtful and loving gestures are the mechanisms for the greatest romance on this side of the ghetto.

Her family complains that she is going down emotionally and materially, but she is in denial. "He is the only one in my life who is helping me to make it. We will get on our feet soon. None of you understand what this man has been through. He is a father to my children, a friend and lover to me, and is willing to be a friend to all of you, if you let him. He is constantly looking for work but there is no job in his field. Plus with a record behind him, the system works against him. His wife is trying to break us up. He doesn't want her but she manipulates him because of their children. We could have more but she has the audacity to ask for child support, knowing what his situation is. I'm almost glad that he is unemployed–that way they can't take all of his earnings. Yes, he gets frustrated and hits me sometimes, but that's not all the time. Usually he is sweet, loving, and so helpful when he is not depressed. People tend to mess with him and that upsets him. I'm closest so he takes it out on me but we are working on his temper. One thing I can say about the man is that he knows how to apologize."

I wish I could say that this story is unique but it isn't. A lot of women are looking for love in all the wrong places. It does not matter that stop signs, red lights, hazard signs, road block signs, dangerous chemical signs, condemned signs, proceed with caution signs, and beware of signs are posted to help us avoid faulty relationships. And yet, we continue to find our thrill from someone else's home, over the state line, down in the blueberry field, behind the gate, in the alley, boardrooms, and you name it, we can claim it.

When will common sense kick in? When will some women remember that they do not need a man to feel good about themselves? When will they know that a man will find the woman who has respect, fulfillment, knowledge, creativity and humor? When will they look beyond making a man happy without regards to their own happiness? When will foolish women stop traveling to prisons and rehabilitations to find a mate that they believe God told them to take? Wouldn't it be simpler for a mighty God to create a man outside of the penal system, who will appreciate a woman, and work physically, spiritually, and mentally to bring the best into both of their lives?

When will all this madness end? Even in old age, foolish women abound. Maybe when age has taken control of our physical needs and reduced our sexual capacity to a point where we proclaim "I have a dream of what it used to be like." Can you imagine a woman saying, "There was a time when I was fine–like splendid wine? I had a figure that couldn't wait–when every man in town had his eye on me–fell at my feet–and told me it was fate. Those were the days!" When we said we had a "man," trust me, we had one or they were set free. There is no moral standard of living that is healthy and whole for women who have not learned to nurture before the relationship develops. If they don't learn appropriately, life will teach them that nothing from nothing leaves nothing but heartache and stress.

Freedom Begins With You!

Here you are, in jail again. Why do you do it? Why do you leave your family defenseless and alone without your presence? Why do you choose to leave me, a young woman in my prime, to lie alone in my bed at night? Alone and afraid because I don't want to live without you. I don't want to be by myself, raising our children without a father.

Why do you come home from incarceration, looking for a handout from relatives and friends, preying on the innocent and blaming others for your situation? Who promised you a rose garden in the ghetto, a fairy tale life, different from the one you created? The rest of us get up and go to work to earn our living–we made a choice. You had the same choices, same opportunity, same family, and similar experiences. We are no more and no less than you but you think at "ground level" and the forces of good can't bring you up to a "higher thought process."

Why do you steal, cheat, and lie without a valid reason? Anything, it seems, to block your progress. I get tired of explaining to the children that "daddy's in trouble again, but it is not his fault. Once again, he has been framed by somebody who had a grudge against him or it may be mistaken identity. Pray for him to be released soon." I refuse to take them to the jail again and watch them try to reach through the glass in order to touch your hands–to be close to you. How dare you expose them to this kind of life, not to mention me? A life of crime that ultimately drains you emotionally and physically, causes so many scars, and seems so hopeless to anyone with common sense. After we leave the jail, it is I who wipe their tears, calm their fears, and explain your innocence. It is I, who will cover up and make your lifestyle more suitable, so that they will retain some form of affection for you in the future. You need to understand life is not a game designed by the systems that exist to you. Your children are more mature and wiser. I refuse to continue to play this same old game forever. I, too, am getting older and wiser to the facts of our life.

At home, you are restless and looking for a fast dollar rather than teaching your sons that education and hard work are the basis for their success. You should be teaching them that "you don't give up, you don't give out, and you don't give in, to temptation that may destroy your life. You stick it out, for the sake of those who love you."

I'm tired of waiting, tired of courtrooms, tired of being mama and daddy too. I have a right to be tired, when I am supposed to have a man, healthy and strong, to take care of me. I deserve a man who remembers that God helps the man that has a job of his own–one that I promised on our wedding day, to love, cherish, and obey. Why won't you give up your selfish desires for us? Why won't you change and let us love you? What can I say but "good-bye" until your choices match the lifestyle that your family must have to prosper? Don't ever forget that you had true love from a strong, committed woman and the pride of your children before you closed the door on your second-chance at love and spiritual rebirth.

Is The Man of the House At Home?

So you want to be a man! A breadwinner. A father. You state that you can handle all of the responsibilities that make a man a man. Help yourself. All the people want to know is "Is the man of the house home?" It's no use telling a woman to be a female educator if you're unwilling to be the strong common denominator. Jesse Jackson stated that "fools can make babies. You're a man only if you can raise a baby, protect a baby, and provide for a baby."

A real daddy, in spite of the mother's attitudes and behavior, looks forward to the challenge of parenthood. Even though he may feel that he was not asked to make the decision to have a child, he tells all who listen that this child is a part of me. It's a part of me that I can see in features and characteristics. Whether I'm happy or sad, humble or proud, rejected or neglected, that does not affect the love which I possess for my child.

Those fathers who want to stand up and be counted need to hear the words of Martin Luther King III, son of slain Civil Rights Leader, Martin L. King II. He said, "The ultimate test of a man is not where he stands on positions of comfort and convenience but where he stands on positions of challenge and controversy." For example: You may suspect that the child in your home may not be your own, especially if you listen to well-meaning friends. You ought to care enough to share love with those within your household and keep the deceivers on the outside trying to break up somebody else's domicile.

What kind of life style do you maintain for the future of your family? What preparations for your children's future have you made? Are you willing to feed your family and be responsible as the man of the house? Can some of you give up a life of crime and immorality to promote the potential and respect which your family requires? Will you look beyond pleasure and a con to see a family who needs a father just as others do?

Your children have an inherent desire to look upon you with pride. To see beyond a welfare check and view trust bending over backwards, pulling weeds if necessary, to feed them beans. They deserve a home and not a halfway house to merely exist. It would please them to go to bed and rise early in the morning without a fight. To see food and milk in the refrigerator rather than liquor.

You're a man! Prove it to yourself and those who love you. Say to yourself, "If I steal, then nothing I do is real. If I kill the will, I can claim the victory. Nothing comes before me that I cannot handle. I must take charge because I cannot afford to harm the small replicas of myself." It is time out for games and human lotteries. Only the strong survive and it is rare to find a Prince alone in the jungles of life. You're a man! You're somebody special, molded by God, created to lead. Women will follow if the leader shows love, power, and endurance. We will survive because we did not come this far alone. We need you and you need us.

When you can pass the drugs, shun the liquor, smile at the con artists headed for never ever land, deny the street image, and defy the gangster, while you whisper "Peace" to the unbelievers, then you have begun to recognize the unlimited resources you possess to make it.

You're a man! When you can show it, the world will know it. You can be a daddy if your mind says " I am a daddy!" You can't do anything about your past mistakes. We've all been guilty. We can choose this day to change our lives. The question is, "Is the man of the house at home?" Somebody will one day say "Who is that man?" And your children will shout "That's my daddy!"

When You Are Black, Tell Me Where is Your Hope for the Future?

In the newspaper, on the radio, and the focus of the majority of magazines, the stereotype Black personality is described in the most derogative portrayal that can be found. The human despair may cause various reactions among the masses of human beings who try to interpret the rationale for the depictions.

African American citizens of this United States of America are the least represented, the least respected, the least selected, and the least expected to succeed. They are the first to be rejected, the first neglected, the first inspected, the last ones expected to arrive, and the first one's suspected. Make no mistake that the color of one's skin carries a strong message. A message that reminds the sender and the receiver that "You are an exception to the rule. That you may be a part of this project but you are also the object of scrutiny."

Of course, the cities will tell you that all women face the same barriers, that Jews are also hated, that Hispanics are discriminated against, that homosexuals are alienated, and even cite the white male as an endangered species. However, when you get to the heart of the matter, the consensus is that any person, group, or nationality is preferable to being Black. This statement does not call for research and statistics; but is based on facts from daily living experiences.

Individuals of most races can blend with society in language and cultural changes, but if you are considered and determined to be Black, at some point you will be reminded by a look, exclusion, some comment or definition, or denied for some recognized event or work participation. This society wonders why drugs and alcohol are so pervasive in the Black Community. Wake up, understand and seek the truth! Understand that all human beings arrived in the world by similar means. It was the intense observations and future learned perceptions that helped to create the end result. See your factories, your shuttered businesses, your new assessments for promotions, and the double standards used by the financial institutions, the educational institutions and medical facilities; and ask this generation to account for a better way and a greater day.

Tell them, the black males and females, that they have the same opportunities as the rest of society. Tell them that they have the chance to advance beyond an assistantship or Vice President position, if they work harder then others on the job. Explain to them how they must be careful when they become the "first" in government, in sports, in entertainment, in education, and any other field; the fact that they represent not only themselves but a whole race of people.

Explain to them about dope in the inner city which may have come from the suburbs. Explain that money becomes mama and power becomes papa. Explain why history denied a heritage of pride to be told, though it described slavery, and why Blacks deserve at least one free ride, if there is positive transition going out of the valley of despair to the top of the mountain. Explain how society now demands birth control when it once dared this race to have a conscience and soul to even question the number of births. Explain to children who stand on the corners how they were bought and sold on corners for far less than they could even equate. Tell them that there is true equality and that changes will come, because you, the silent majority, are willing to break down the barriers of indifference and hate. Tell them that the racial jokes and subtle racism tactics will end in your place of business, the social events you plan–and mean it!

Explain to them about a terrible city with controversial leaders, school boards with in-house tensions and streets crying with the blood of our youth. Tell them that you care enough to stop looking for negatives and are building for the positives that exist within your city. You see, if you tell a child that he's bad for a length of time, it has been proven that he will begin to believe and live by that concept. That child will begin to emulate behaviors and attitudes that support what has been repeated to them over and over again. A self-fulling prophecy will perpetuate itself without assistance. There is no one in power who has the right to make their own laws against the wishes of the constituents. No wrongful deeds by any leader should be condoned, regardless of race, although the judgements truly lie with those of power.

"It's difficult to tell me where my hope for the future lies, when you hold the keys of opportunity and won't allow me to open up one door to satisfy my curiosity, as I've seen done for countless others. Don't let me be the exception, allow me to be the rule."

Why Martin Luther King Jr. Day?

Why Martin Luther King Day? Why not Elvis Presley Day? Yeah, and why not Italian Day? Yea, and why not Jewish Day? Why not Rosa Park's Day? Yea, and why not a day for the Beatles? Ok, we're building the fire of confusion!

What? What are you all fussing about? Some people don't deserve this day? What did they do that was significant? Let me tell you something. You don't know anything. These people deserve a national holiday. Listen to what they did:

<u>Elvis Presley</u> told us in a song not to touch his blue suede shoes and to jail house rock–he was good but not good enough to stand for justice of the poor and racism of the minorities.

<u>Italians</u> are great people but they have been recognized by history and can pass the race test without any major problems. Every day is their day to be blessed and recognized for their talents..

<u>Hispanics</u> are beautiful people with that exciting bilingual ability. They, too, understand the pain of racism and what stereotypes will do to alienate one individual from another. With the ability to communicate effectively, they can go where they choose and find acceptance, if the money and opportunity seem to be adequate. They can say "I am from South America, from Mexico City, or New Mexico; to name a few and somehow blend in.

Jews are some of the most intelligent, most resourceful people on earth. They have suffered so much and yet they too, can command respect and pass through the system if they choose to change a name or be silent about their heritage. Economically, they have learned to " make their money and property talk for them" to the powers of this world despite the prejudice directed towards their nationality. They can name their day.

Rosa Parks was a good woman but her main reason for standing boldly in the face of racism that day in Alabama was because she was tired. That incident sparked by Rosa caused the Civil Rights Movement to gain more momentum and others across the nation joined the struggle. No one will ever deny or take her glory. This was her season to be blessed. She has had her day and has shared many more.

The Beatles told us in song that "we've had a hard day and night–that we've been working like dogs." They taught us that people may laugh at first but your talent and ability would gain you respect. Their days were many and the world gave them great honor, with screams and tears of adulation. As they lived and died, they were celebrated by the media and the world for what they accomplished through music.

What did Martin Luther King do? Martin Luther King Jr. was not self-centered. He was a Moses who told America "To let my people go." He walked, he marched, he talked, he loved, he forgave, he tried to save, he prayed, and he sung. He was abused and he was accused. He was hosed and he was chose. He was attacked and he was tracked. He made it possible to sit at the front of the bus. He made it possible to go to schools where you choose. He made it possible to sleep in the finest hotel and deny a wrong to prevail. He made it possible to vote and to borrow on a promissary note. He made it possible to have pride without getting a free ride. He gave each of us, all people, all races, all nationalities, all religions, all genders, a personal right to hope, and to dream. We inherited the power to look beyond the dream and visualize reality, not just to have a commonality but to exude with energy and a vibrant personality. He made it possible for us to view death from a mountain top experience and to glimpse victory in the promise of God's Word.

Like Moses he did not live to see his dreams materialize here on earth, but on his day, Martin Luther King Day, we remember him. We remember that he did not die just for Blacks but for all people who are oppressed and denied human rights. This man deserves a day not because he's African American or Black, if you will, but because he earned the right. If he were alive today, he would say, "I could care less about a day. Show me an individual who has not received respect and justice and I will give you a day of my life." However, those who reaped the promises he fought for and can enjoy the privileges so long denied, are the ones who dare to say "Why not a day for one so deserving?"

Who can equal these humanitarian words from Dr. King who boldly said to American society, "I have the audacity to believe that people everywhere can have three meals a day for their bodies, education and culture for their minds, and dignity, equality, and freedom for their spirit. I believe that what self-centered men have torn down, other centered men can build up." I will choose to serve others in the community on my holiday off. What will you do?

Chapter 4

Strong Women of Adversity in Times Like These

Standing on the Promises of God!

Do you have any idea how precious you are? Do you know that God has a blessing for you that no one can take away? Have you grasped the meaning of a crucified Jesus dying so that you might have everlasting life and the freedom to meet your deliverance with a smile? Have you any idea that an Angel of the Lord has been dispatched to stand and watch over you in your midnights as well as your victories?

If not, let me assure you today that I discovered that I am not poverty stricken in the faith. I have learned that God is on my side. He woke me one morning, early one morning–just about the break of day–to remind me that "there is a balm in Gilead." He wanted me to recognize my purpose in my praise and service. I listened as the Holy Spirit admonished me to read and hear the words that would set me free.

You see, I have been praying for God to bless areas of my life. He has already prepared the foundation. My problem is that I need to understand my purpose in the preparation. He wants me to have great things because I deserve great things as a representative of the Kingdom. I have learned that I am an anointed child of the kingdom and should be able to walk with kings and queens. I ought to be able to sit in the presence of friends in high places and to know that I have a right to expect all that comes with it.

What we have done is limit ourselves to receive less than the best because the traditional church has told us not to aspire for abundance because "that is being carnal-minded and as such, is an abomination to God." What we fail to remember is that God has made promises to us and without a purpose or faith in His Word, we cannot claim them. We are heirs and recipients of wealth and prosperity. Did not the scriptures teach us in Phil 4:19 that "God will supply all of our needs according to His riches in glory?" Did not the Apostle Paul say that "we have not because we ask not?" Did not John 14:14 say that "we can ask anything in Jesus' name and it would be done?"

Did not John in the 15th chapter teach us about the "True vine and abiding in the word of God? Did it not detail what God would do if we ask anything in the name of His Son Jesus?"

I am trying to grasp what God desires of me and the truth of the matter is that I am somewhat afraid. You might be wondering why and I suppose I am still uncertain. I can only surmise that to have a greater calling would put me in direct confrontation with expectations of those around me. I love a challenge but there is a deeper calling on my life to make a difference in the lives of others by my testimony and doing the will of my Father. The world does not know me and I have difficulty knowing the worldly side of life. Before you ask, let me assure you that I have not become a saint who judges others harshly–that is not my intent. I am striving to be better because I have been richly blessed.

I have played the games that people play and been loved and unloved, hugged and shrugged, played and strayed, made and weighed, and yet, I still stand. I have been standing with tongues lashing at my heels and wanting to give up but afraid of the consequences of saying "I give up." I have invited suicide to talk with me and mess with my head but I still stand. I have drunk from the cup of rejection, too bitter to swallow and yet, I still stand. I have heard the lightening and the thunder of relationships roll but I still stand. I have seen the degradation, premeditation and unrepentant conciliation cross my path and observed the garbage truck of despair pick up my lost dreams and hopes and dump them by the wayside. I have been at the Master's feet of forgiveness and begged to be restored. Like David "I asked to be washed and made whole." I wanted God to restore unto me my missing joy because apart from Him I am not happy. I have been miserable and disillusioned at the prospect of being without my "first love"–Jehovah God.

Can you imagine being without your mouth, your feet, your mind, your intimate parts, your eyes, your nose, your arms and hands, your face? Oh, what love the Father had for me. Can't you see it? He took me from nowhere, placed me somewhere peaceful, and made me to lie down in green pastures of righteousness. He gave me water that was not from the well and nurtured me with food that I did not plant. Who is it that can take my purpose and tell me who I am and where I belong? For unless they can love me better and treat me with the respect I now expect–they can keep "stepping" while I keep "pressing toward the mark of a higher calling."

I have a vision and a plan developing in my mind that will move me toward my goal. With God all things are possible and I have to believe that what was promised will come, special delivery, with my name embossed on it so there will be no mistaken identity of the recipient. There will be a knock on the door of my heart and I will answer. The blessing will be delivered and the messenger will receive my signature made up of thanks and praises. Of course, I have to thank Him as we thank those who are sent to bring our blessings by way of the cross. But my "shout" is ready for I know that God heard me call His name so many times. My request is that I am not forgotten as I move through this life of trials. I want to receive my blessings when they are passed out. I will thank Him for opening up the windows of heaven and showering down blessings too numerous to count.

Listen to the victory and testimony: Before I can close the door, another knock and a repeat performance. Keep listening because before I can close the door–over and over–and over again–God keeps the deliveries coming, just like He promised. Every tear, every heartache, every lie, every cheat, every pain, every stain, every grief, every wrong, every rejection, every burden, every problem–my God paid for it all.

You ask me, what am I doing? I'm standing on the promises of God for He has never promised anything that He is not willing to deliver. My arms are outstretched, with the palms facing up, in order for the gifts of love to overflow. I am willing to move over and make room for you to do the same. Can you see what I see? Can you hear what I hear? If not, take the Bible and ask for a word! There is an answer for those who heed the call.

What Life Didn't Provide, Mother Had in the Love of Her Children

My personal testimony is a living one of my Mother. I am who I am today because my mother, Maggie Lee, lived. She gave birth to fifteen babies and looked well for her labor. I am the second oldest and the eldest girl, therefore, my role was already carved into the family tree. I watched mother love and be-refused, smile and be-accused, and dance-to-the down-south-blues. She was used and abused, but seldom soothed and wooed like a woman appreciated by the men in her life. I guess you could say that "she looked for love in all the wrong places."

Mother was married to my biological father, J.W. Carson, in Prarie, Mississippi and they had four children which included me. Ironically, none of us have ever seen or heard from our father. My mother obtained her divorce, to my knowledge, after newspaper announcements regarding the pending action. Between marriages, my mother had four children by different fathers and she allowed two of them to live with alternate families who were not related to us. None of them were legally adopted. I never understood the rationale for her decisions to conceal the births, other than the fact that she was warned not to birth any more children or she would lose her welfare benefits. I believe that this might account for the different last names on the birth certificates (according to some of my siblings who received theirs and were puzzled.) In those days, children dared not question parents about sex, pregnancies, and other decisions they made and live to explain it. I will admit that I was hurt and confused by the decisions made by mother but loved her with a childlike devotion of acceptance.

One day I came home from school and a strange man was there for dinner. My stepfather had come to visit our mother and never left. They began to have children and continued at a rapid pace until a total of seven children were born which gave us a grand total of fifteen. My grandmother disputed that number and declared that mother had lost more than she indicated but Mother denied it. I watched our Mother go from a care-free, beautiful woman to a battered wife who drank to survive. She would make excuses for black eyes and bruises after she returned from his offers to take her for a ride. One famous excuse was " I ran into a door." My brother Willie and I would be so angry but were unable to challenge her statements. All I knew was anger and grief because as a youngster, I could not protect her from the beatings.

By the time I got to the age of twelve or thirteen, I noticed my stepfather's attention on me and I felt very uncomfortable. Primarily because I was fully developed and aware that some parts of my physical anatomy were drawing a lot of stares from men. One time in particular, I remember my mother going into the hospital to deliver a baby. I was terribly afraid when night came for some unknown reason. As children we slept three or more to a bed and I woke up in the middle of the night to find myself alone with my stepfather trying to rape me. He had removed the sleeping children from the bed. I fought and struggled desperately but quietly, so I would not wake the others. I managed to get away from him but to do so meant that I hid in a closet all night. The next two days, I avoided him and hid in the closet until our mother was released from the hospital. He never attempted to bother me again and I was so grateful to God or whoever it was protecting me. My mother had evidently observed his watching me and she told me one day to "stay out of his face." That hurt me so bad because she never knew that I was trying to get enough courage to tell her of his efforts to rape me. I decided not to say anything because she probably would blame me and not believe what I had to say. Years later, I told both of them the truth, after hearing my stepfather call mother horrible, profane names, and he denied the accusation and called me a liar. She apologized to me for her words and told me that I should have told her. I still think that I made the right decision for that time in my life and hers. Needless to say, my stepfather began a bitter campaign of hatred and vengeance against me that ultimately ended in tragedy.

I got married at nineteen and my house became the home away from home for my mother and my siblings when the violent beatings increased. In order to prevent the state from removing my siblings from the home, I agreed to get her welfare check and pay the bills, including buying the groceries. As a result, my stepfather hated me more and treated Mother worse. The more beatings she received, the more liquor she drank. The children were becoming anxious, fearful, and afraid and called me often to come and get them.

One of my brothers, who was seventeen years old and a popular football star of the local high school, had come to live with me because my mother asked me to take him because of threats from my stepfather. I did so and he became a part of my family. Making the transition was not difficult for either of us, since he always had a special affection for his eldest sister. As a matter of fact, when I gave birth to my first child, he slipped into the hospital room (14 years old), to hold my hand. To make a long story short, I received a call one day from my siblings, requesting me to come and get them because they were hungry and there had been a fight. When I arrived, they all came out of the house and I proceeded to back out of the driveway. My mother ran out of the house and stopped me by jumping into my back seat and landing on top of the children. She screamed that my stepfather had a gun and was going to kill her. Before I could react, he came to the car and pointed the gun at her. All I could think of was my mother and the safety of the children as I got out of the car and tried to reason with him. I had no idea at that time that I was his main target. I am alive today because my brother who was seventeen happened to come by and saw what was happening. He also tried to talk to my stepfather and as he got closer, my stepfather started shooting. Willie C. was shot in the chest and ran across the street where he fell.

Chaos ensued as the children screamed and I and two of my siblings, Rosa and Jessie, managed to hold my stepfather down in a struggle for our lives. We fought on the ground as he struck my sister Rosa on the head with the gun and continued to fire at me until the bullets were gone. There had to be angels there that day because not one bullet aimed hit another person other than my brother. All of the bullets passed me and I look back and marvel at the power of God and His salvation. We held him until the police arrived. I learned later that my death and my mother's were planned months before then and the caseworker at DSS knew of it but did not believe it to be a valid threat. The worker disclosed to me that he did not take the threats serious.

After the police arrived, I discovered that my precious brother, Willie C. Carson, was dead on arrival and our lives had changed. My stepfather went to prison and we saw our mother yield to a life of depression and alcoholism. She gave one of my cousins custody of four of my siblings without consulting any of her older children. They stayed with my cousin for two years until she informed the DSS that she could not keep them any longer. When they called me to see if I would take them, my husband and I did not hesitate to become their guardians. We offered them a life style of religious teaching, regular meals, clean clothing, safe shelter, education, nurturing, and discipline.

As the girls matured, so did their determination to break free of the rules and discipline we required. I frequently heard comments like "you are not our mother, you are our sister. This is like a prison." Conflict between us continued to escalate and my husband and I finally agreed to allow the two older sisters to live with Mother. This would also give her more stability and a monthly check to pay for housing and utilities. I wanted so badly to keep the family together until they all graduated from high school but I consoled myself with the fact that my husband and I tried. I wanted my siblings to experience a better way of living without daily crises and human dramas. I wanted them to have decent food and clean beds. To experience religious renewal and revivals and grow with God who would give them the strength and resources to fight the issues of life. I wanted them to have the support and appreciation that I had not always received. I felt such inner pain and a sense of failure for a long time. Here I was, a young woman, wife and mother, who wanted to make a difference, but without any formal parenting skills or degrees in human psychology. There were few people in my life that I could share how I really felt and who would guide me in my own esteem needs and this time was no exception.

I suppose that I should have related several tragedies that occurred to mother while the children lived with me. One day, the city police detectives, who knew my family, phoned me at work and asked me to come to the hospital right away. They informed me that my mother had been hospitalized for several days as a result of a near death beating from some unknown person or persons. The surgeons wanted to discuss with family members her condition. She had to have total facial reconstruction, because of a broken nose, total breakage of bones in her face, loss of her right eye, loss of all teeth and broken ribs. She moved in with us because no one else had the time or ability to keep her. As she healed, I learned that her friends were sneaking liquor into our home and her drinking became a problem. She got angry when confronted and moved with some of her drinking buddies. Not long after that, I got a call from her friend who informed me that Mother was in the hospital and was very ill. She had intestinal cancer and had to have a colostomy. Again, she had to move in with me until she healed enough to leave. Angels were still protecting her because after six months, the doctor was able to reverse the procedure which allowed her to use her bowels again. Unfortunately the drinking never stopped.

I was tired of her going from house to house and being mistreated because of her addiction. We got a promise from mother that she was going to give up alcohol and do better. This more than anything caused me to allow my sisters, who were both in high school, to move in with Mother so that they could help to care for her. The situation with drinking did not improve and the girls began to call me about mother's activities. I continued to rescue them, talk to mom, cried and prayed. I must admit that I did more crying than anything.

One Saturday afternoon, I will never forget, I got a call from the girls that Mother had a knife and was talking crazy as she waved it at them. I had to attend a church meeting and was responsible for the devotion. I remember vividly crying out to God that it was in His hands because I could not handle it anymore. "Whatever is your will, Lord, let it be done." Later that evening, I attended a gospel music service in the city and received a call to hurry to the hospital. The caller said that my Mother had been struck by a car on the icy streets of Martin Luther King, Jr. Drive. When I arrived at the hospital, I learned that her body was broken in so many places that it was doubtful whether or not she would survive or walk again. It took six months in Berrien General Hospital rehabilitation ward and intensive physical therapy in order for her to come home with mobility.

This time, we observed her progress cautiously and feared that being in her home environment would motivate the urge to drink.

We found to our amazement that God had finally gained a witness of His goodness and mercy. Maggie Lee was finally free to be all that she could be. For eleven more years, God gave us a mother who had freedom from alcohol, abuse, and stress. She joined the church, loved her pastor, and forbid liquor in her apartment. We had family dinners and laughed together. I told all of my siblings that no matter what others said about our mother, we would hold our heads high and love her. We promised to respect her for the mother she was now rather than where she had been in the past.

In April of 1989, a year of turmoil for my husband and I, our home burned down. In June of that same year, my mother was diagnosed with cancer of the throat as a result of excessive smoking. She was in a critical stage when I took her to a throat specialist. They were unable to save her voice and could not give her a voice box implant. She had a tracheotomy in her throat which she depended on. The doctor learned that she had difficulty breathing without it. Our Mother loved to talk and this change in her life was a big defeat for her. I learned later that she refused to have the physician tell our family of her terminal condition. Someone had to be with her 24 hours a day which became a challenge for those of us who were committed to caring for her. We should have known the status of her health but I think we were too afraid to ask or to believe that this was a possibility. I attended all of her appointments with her, therefore, I was aware of her treatment and care. One day, I remember hearing the physician speak to her in a tone which I believed to be less than respectful and I waited to confront to him.

I said to him "Doctor, maybe to you, this woman is a poor, black woman, illiterate and unable to speak but I am here to represent her. If you have a question and she cannot answer it, I am a professional person and qualified to tell you what you want to know. If not, let me comprehend what she is trying to say and explain it to you. If she can't understand you–talk to me. She has been through too much and nobody, not you or anyone else, will talk to her with less than the respect she deserves. Thank you for taking care of my mother." Needless to say, his whole demeanor changed and he nurtured her each time she came. He was wonderful to her. On Christmas Day, in 1989, Mother died. She told all of us prior to her death that "everything would be all right." She made her peace with God. She was unable to speak verbally but she would raise her arms and mouth the words. What a mighty God we serve!

Losing my mother, my sister, my friend and often, my daughter in recent years, was one of the most painful seasons of my life. She told me several days before her death to sit down so that she could talk to me and I did. I learned more about my mother that day than any other time in my life. The interesting thing about our conversation was that I really had to listen because I had to read her lips. She would write a note if I could not understand her. I learned of her southern upbringing and the challenges she endured. She told me frightening stories of her life here in Michigan. I had tears in my eyes when she said that she had never been truly loved by any man in spite of the number of children she had borne. According to her, grandmother, who raised her, never loved her or appreciated her. All she remembered being called were names like "trifling" and "no good." I, too, remember hearing my mother called names as well as my other siblings because we were often the poorest or the homeless of the family. Mother stated that she always loved and wanted grandmother's approval but never got it. Those days are in the past and I grew to love my great-grandmother and I knew that she loved me and my siblings.

What else can I say? A whole lot more, but I'll save that for my speeches to troubled women who need a word of encouragement from someone who has been there and done that. My mother left a legacy and when I see my brothers and sisters who are survivors of the streets, hunger, addictions, and violence, I tell God, "thank you." Look where God has brought us. It is up to us to break the cycle of loveless relationships, drug abuse, child abuse, spouse abuse, homelessness, joblessness, child neglect, hatefulness, jealousy, irresponsibility, and fear. We belong to a royal family who are tired of being victims of circumstances. Tired of being mistreated and carriers of hurt and pain that is so deep-seated. Tired of pretending that happiness is having nothing and nothing is a product of a big something that is coming. We are overcomers, anointed and blessed. We have been tested and resurrected, neglected and perfected, but it is all good because what the devil meant for evil God meant for good.

After this testimonial about my mother, do you wish you could have met her? If you do, I have a thought: There are ten of us still living and as you see, and hear all ten of us, you are seeing Maggie Lee in each of us, male and female. I believe we have the character and the integrity to make it through times such as these. Hard times build character if you are in sync with God. Determination will become a foundation of strength when you allow faith to dwell where love has begun a spiritual work within the soul. I can witness, can you?

How to Overcome the Odds & Make Positive Things Happen for You

1. <u>Start With the Little Things.</u> Take your problems one day at a time and learn to accept your human frailties as a barrier that can be removed with time and planning.

2. <u>Recognize the Power of Time.</u> Time cannot be measured or saved for an appropriate season. You will meet time sitting down, prostrate, or standing up. I propose that we meet it, head on, fearless and confident that our hope lies in the plans of tomorrow.

3. <u>Appreciate Your Heritage.</u> Don't keep hiding behind your failures (broken relationships, financial losses, old hurts, family alienation, environmental disappointments and even your sorrow). Remember individuals (your role models) in your life or community who knew you when you did not know yourself in a positive sense, and realize that they are your pages of history. Take the yokes of knowledge and continue to learn of those who paved the way for you.

4. <u>Be All That You Can Be.</u> How many times do you receive praise for the good things you do? You are right! They seldom share positive things that you do or say with you. Somehow people seem to feel more comfortable expressing negatives rather than positives which can be elevate our self-esteem. Some <u>good</u> advice is to tell your self that you are not going to surrender your values nor your peace of mind that you are capable and qualified. Know that you have been educated in the high school and college of hard knocks. You graduated with a PhD in <u>Prayer</u>, <u>Hunger</u> and <u>Determination</u>. Praise yourself and <u>always</u> praise others.

5. <u>Don't Take No for An Answer?</u> Do you think the world cares whether you make it or not? Do you really believe that your concerns become paramount problems of everyone who knows you? You are dreaming! Wake up and live. Consider your consequences and if the answer <u>needs</u> to be "<u>no</u>" then do not hesitate to do so. However, if opportunity reaffirms your potential to obtain something valuable in the process, run swiftly to your reward for you deserve the best. Haven't you been tried and found to be steadfast?

6. <u>The Power of self-talk is tremendous.</u> When we can say to ourselves that we are okay, we are. When we can tell ourselves that we are capable and lovable, then we are. When we can tell those around us that we are beautiful and know without a doubt that there is <u>inner</u> as well as an <u>outer</u> beauty, we can make it.

7. <u>Too often other people are needlessly hurt because they fail to recognize the power that lies within the spirit.</u> It is important to know where you started from in order to determine where you are going. Dialogue with yourself so that there is emotional balance in the problem solving process.

8. <u>Do not be afraid to dream.</u> Positive things just don't happen. Not perfect marriages–Not perfect children nor homes nor jobs. There are no perfect schools and no perfect religious. Everything starts with a dream and with nurturing and motivation becomes reality. One day Martin Luther King, Jr., had a dream and the doors of freedom began to open. But they didn't just open. He mobilized his efforts with other movers and shakers and with action required determination, and with determination came power and the scenario evolved in victory.

How strong are you? Test yourself . . . Look at what you do well . . . Think positive about your strengths and your weaknesses. You can fool everyone for a time but seldom can you fool yourself. Tell the truth about yourself, where you are going and how you plan to get there.

Do you have a mule or thoroughbred philosophy?

<u>Mule Philosophy</u> - means that you must be prodded and pushed to move

forward in your life. You depend on goals of others to promote your happiness, but alas! If they don't succeed . . .

Thoroughbred Philosophy - means that you are in the race to win. You dare not find peace, happiness, nor love, solely in another individual because victory is only in the perseverance of the optimist who will not quit. After all, the race isn't given to the swift and neither to the strong, but to those, who will endure until the end.

Watch Me!

Watch me as I rise from the mess I've made of my life. See me hold my head up as I soar to heights unknown to you and those who counted me among the lost souls of despair. Oh yes, I know you gave up on me as a woman, victorious in my struggle to survive. What you did not know then and must not know now is that I have felt the pain and initialed my scars so that I will not forget what brought me to this moment. Watch me and see the evidence of my breakthrough.

I want you to see me crawl through my degradation and intimidation to reach my self-determination and meditation. Watch me as I overcome obstacles, too numerous to mention, in order to be all that I plan to be. There is no limit to my success just as there was no limit to the "mess" in my life. Every day is a new day, a new beginning, a new challenge, and a testimony of my faith.

Watch me closely–those who dare to believe that I have not survived appropriately, by your standards, for it will be you that will witness my breakthrough to victory. You will tell my story for me and with excitement, praise my virtue and the multitude of experiences you have seen me survive. It will be you who will defend my honor when demonic forces come against me. You will stand boldly to proclaim my innocence even though the negatives appear to outweigh my positives.

Watch me because God said he would not have me put to shame. You will see me cleanse myself of the past which stole a portion of my youth and my inheritance. It stole my thoughts, my passion, my appearance, my purpose, and attempted to invade my soul. At that point, I knew that I had to make a choice of life or death. Watch me as I mandate a stronghold on my peace of mind, with or without others in my corner. This war within must be fought by me on my terms and not that of the enemy. I recognize that my greatest battle will be fought within. It is the inner person that longs to be possessed and caressed, redressed without stress, but I shall control what goes in and what comes out. This is my eminent domain and I refuse to sell out to the aggressor. God will design the way to make my life desirable and prosperous.

Watch me as I show you my compassion which before I would ration, rather than give freely to another. Watch me live my renewed faith and redefined strength though you have to lean close for the knowledge. You see me smile through my pain but you have not seen my shame nor shared my blame. Only those who saw me slide in the night time and moan in the day time know what I have suffered. Only a look will remind me of the blessing I have obtained to be here today. My blessings are overtaking me as I share with you my breakthrough. I cannot go back–I have to go forward. I cannot bow down–I must reach higher. I cannot give up–I have to live up to the standards set by the Savior. I cannot be discouraged–I have courage beyond my power. I cannot be embarrassed–God cherished with love this woman in spite of her past. I am no longer hungry for the world–because I am fed by the Word of God.

Watch me as I live up to standards that I know will keep me free and steadfast. Watch with me for just a little while as I learn to run this life with patience. I see a vision and there is a miracle attached to the view. I am expecting a new creature to continually emerge from the valley of despair to the mountain of wealth. I have to see it or I cannot possess it. I have to believe it or I cannot accept it. I know it is there because the promise has already been provided in the scriptures, over and over again. Watch me and see if I will make a believer of you. You know what? You haven't seen anything yet!

Is Anything Too Hard for God?

Alienated, isolated and frustrated, you look for reasons to get up in the morning; a reason to function in an imperfect world. You seek for love in all the wrong places. Your choices are based on emotion rather than logic. You want to give up and by all intent and purpose, do so.

A mature and lovely woman like you, alone and despondent–what went wrong? But if you could answer that question, you would know the solution and pull yourself free of horrible feelings. A marriage, a relationship gone bad and a secret known to few–one of abuse in a "thought to be" perfect home. What do you do? How do you tell the church where you both worship throughout the week and hold leadership roles that you are both miserable people? Do you admit that you teach love and the wonderful works of God and yet don't believe that God can salvage your union? Both you and your mate play the loving family role so well that you are envied for the glow that never changes. You've prayed for guidance and it seems that God is still saying "wait."

God must be able to see the futility of this situation and come down and separate you or at least fix your problem mate. You don't understand why He hasn't done anything that is obvious when you have called His name so many times. Both of you claim the other has issues and you surmise that your mate has the greatest need for counseling. Family and friends are getting suspicious and you begin to make excuses regarding family functions or friendly gatherings. You know that for your mental well-being, something will have to change. Your change is initiated by reading inspirational books and listening to audio tapes on self-empowerment. You convince yourself that you are invincible–a child of the King. Your message to others are positive quotes from leading novelists like Iyanla Vanzant, Steven Kimbro, T.D. Jakes, and Joyce Myers, to name a few. These quotes flow from your mouth as though you are the epitomy of exemplary womanhood. There is a renewed sense of value in your dialogue and the way you wear your esteem.

Tears come in your eyes and down your face, unbidden at times, because you are so frustrated at life's many challenges and the facade you hide behind. Of course, there is nothing wrong with you or your home–that would ruin the scenario. You have an allergy that won't seem to go away. Who, me unhappy? Whatever would I have reason to cry for? You cannot be moved by the things you see nor the things that you hear because nothing is too hard for you. The Lord is faithful to those who believe His Words and are not fearful of His promises. He can Fix anything–make anything brand new. "The Potter can put me back together again" you say with strong conviction. What man sees as defeat–God sees as a receipt. Your debt has been paid in full regardless of what man may say you owe.

The Savior does not need to throw out a lifeline. His Word is the line, the hook and the bait. He can draw your blessings in and soften the adversarial waves that come so strong against you. What is too hard for you is just right for God. Relationships mean so much to us but without the spirit of the Lord to guide us, we forget where our help comes from. When you worry about what family and friends are saying about your situation, remember that they, too, have relationships and stories that do not always want to be told. We are all sinners, saved by grace and privileged to be a witness to what God has done for us. Nothing will ever be too hard for God for He is the creator of all good things. All we have to do is believe that they are ours for the asking. Now wipe your eyes and claim your prize.

God will tell you to look your persecutors in the eye and say "I love you." He will prompt you to tell your accusers "I forgive you." His love will break your hatred down to small pieces of "what can I give to you." He will take the worry out of your tomorrow and allow you to live in peace today. The Word of God is medicine to your soul. Respect the power of it and it will lead you to the throne of Grace. Many times we are taken through things that perplex us and cause us to question our stamina. When we recognize the hand of the Master, we will know that God is in control and will bless us in his own time. Wipe your eyes and get ready for your heavenly hug. God is up there now, wrapping your prayer requests personally. What you thought was too hard has been "just" enough for a sister-in-Christ.

My Premiums Are Paid Up: Where is My Policy?

God will send you a notice regarding your policy of life here on earth. If you are paid up, your benefits will be available when you become a recipient of prayer. The good thing about this policy is that it is not term life so it won't depreciate when you need it. It is whole life and you can draw dividends on it.

Another great blessing is that there are no surprises, such as: let us check back to other years in order to determine whether the policy will pay off. You won't have to contact a lawyer to make the provider pay. The Provider is Jesus Christ of Nazareth and he delivers according to His promises. Listen, our Savior owns everything, therefore he can write us a check on demand.

How do you get a policy? Give your life to Christ, acknowledge your sins and be baptized in his name. Your policy is enforced and your life, based on the love and grace of God, will pay your premiums. The dividends will continue to grow. No one can claim what is rightfully yours for everything is in your name.

Man will lie, cheat, and cancel their claims paid to insure you. You may be ill for a greater period of time than the policy holder anticipated when you apply for benefits paid by you. You will be under suspicion and scrutinized for seeking what is rightfully yours. This will cause you to rejoice rather than to become paranoid and discouraged. Truth and reality will see you through. Every tear, every heartache, every injustice, every lie, told on you, every pain–will bring you added insurance consideration. When you feel the effects of your circumstances, weak though you may be, the policy will fulfill its premise.

Don't cancel your earthly insurance policy because you need the coverage for the benefit of your family. You need this policy because it benefits you and your family. Healing and deliverance will increase the value of your insurance policy. Expect a miracle in out-of-the-way places. You can do that because all of your steps have been ordered by God. Your premium is paid and your policy is ready. All you have to do is remember to stand no matter what comes against you. You may pay and pay without using the benefits but as sure as you live, the need will arise. Be prepared and the love that you have invested, the faith you have placed in reserve, will give you a return that the devil in hell cannot withdraw. He does not have the authority nor the knowledge to cancel what has been stored up for this moment in time. Man cannot touch your policy because it is in a safe deposit box marked "heavenly role call." Only the Trinity can release the benefits at an appointed time.

We ought to be praising God for the victory of knowing that God has our back. What about you? Are you thankful for the unmerited gift that belongs to you? If you are, stay your course and we shall meet at the fountain of blessings, beyond any that the world has ever known.

Sh' Sh', Don't Tell Nobody...

"Hush girl, don't you tell nobody 'bout what happened to you. It wasn't really the worst that could happen. You going to have folks talking 'bout you 'stead of him. So he touched you, put his hand on you, so you said, but you didn't die. You not bruised so it shows and you can walk good, so you'll make it. Before you go telling stuff on people, make sure you got the story right. You know the way you act sometimes, or dress in them short dresses, or talk that "tough street-talk." All of that could have forced the man to do what he did.

You know mama always told us that men are weak to women. When they see women strutting 'round a room, their hearts can't stand the pressure. I'm told their ribs start closing up and they can't be still. Their eyes become glazed and their minds wander. Women shouldn't be mad, 'cause men can't stop bad habits. No body knows what it is that causes this problem. For example: One man said he was at a church minding his own business and a woman with a short dress and "big pretty legs" sat down by him. He said he was sweating and praying at the same time.

He told me that she crossed her legs and you could see the promise land without a rear view mirror. He sung "Swing down Sweet Chariot" and his prayer was "Have mercy Lord." He said that she smiled at him and he inhaled and exhaled a prayer of faith. Service for him was in the pew and the sermon was out the door." But trust me, not one soul will believe that this happens sometimes in spiritual sanctuaries except those who indulge, because this is a sinful practice. It is a power of darkness that keeps us from praising God, although it was a "neon light to me."

Another man, a seasoned man, a self-made man, single man, said he is harassed by women on the job on a regular basis but he will never turn them in. He has a girlfriend and they know it but they continue to flirt with him. According to him, he wears cologne on the job and women go crazy when they smell it. Some whisper as they pass "I can smell you before I see you. One day I'll get you. I can do more for you than she can." He said that he doesn't blush like a woman but women today are bold. Some of the women who flirt are young and he said you have to pray 'cause a brick house ain't saying nothing–they got a whole foundation. He said and I quote "they don't know that they are a lamb with a former wolf on the premises." I have to sing "yield not to temptation" and pray as they walk away. I'm an old man to them but I got fire still in my furnace. Oh, I almost forgot, I got a woman already. But don't tell nobody ok?

Are we to excuse our men when they abuse and demoralize our women? At the same time do we excuse our females who continually provoke men to immoral sexual behavior and pray for their salvation? A man must be a man with morals and principles that he determines are a value to him as well as the society he operates in. There is no such thing as the inability for a man to restrain himself when a woman is in the view, provocative or otherwise. He must be in control and standing tall with respect and moralilty.

A woman must not minimize another woman by rationalizing abuse to her person. Mama and grandma were great people but let's face it; they perpetrated the message "Sh,' Sh,' don't tell nobody." This is our family secret." The black church had a similar message "keep what happens in church behind these walls." And they all said "Amen," but the victims say "Here we go again" and they learn to model the trend.

You Know You've Got a Nerve!

Life is a challenge and so are people. You can die if you want to but not me, I refuse to allow others to get the best of me. Walking around me, putting me down, wanting me to clown and act a fool, not me. You know you got a nerve when you work overtime to make sure I fail at life in general.

You wear a mask depending on who you are with and your face is like a chameleon but I know who you are. I sense your spirit of envy and hate for me though you smile and flatter me with your honey-dipped words. I watch you slip negativity into the conversation whenever I am being complemented. You quickly explain that these are not your opinions but comments that you overheard from others and you wanted me to know. I am reminded constantly that I should slow down because the world will still revolve without me. I feel rather than see your resentment even at church when my name is announced for some service or event. Where do you draw the line? Don't you realize that you will never be blessed appropriately while you spend your time trying to block my blessings? How dare you set yourself up as my judge and jury but refuse me the right to defend myself? At least be honest about your motives.

Let's set the record straight: your job, your home, your marriage, your education, your finances, or any other thing, will not hinder the blessings that belong to me. I cannot jeopardize what belongs to you. I believe in the power of God and what he can do for each of us individually and collectively. You've got a nerve but I have the Word and that defines who and what I am about. Now, take care of your business and allow me to take care of mine.

Praying for Strength When Being a Woman Is Not Enough!

A transformed woman in enemy territory under an assumed identity, traveling incognito, to the promised land of opportunity. Riding on a premise and stranded by a promise, we stand on the threshold of disappointment. God keeps the light of His love shining through so that we can reflect the love that He has demonstrated towards us and yet, we refuse to see the image.

Those who will look and recognize the resemblance will be strengthened in the knowledge that this great God we serve will deliver us from our inner turmoil. However, those of us who do not see the beauty that shines so clearly on our creativity and uniqueness will continually respond to negativity.

Pray for strength when people hate you without a cause. Do not do evil for evil–"vengeance is mine" saith the Lord. Do you comprehend what I am saying? Do you hear the inner person crying out for love and support? My heart is open to the peace and knowledge of God. My depression cannot co-exist with my energetic spirit of life and joy. Why do I keep looking back at yesterday with all of its mistakes and trials when today offers so much more? Satan desires for us to walk around with our heads down, giving up with stress as our companion. He wants us to put our hands up in defeat and yell "I give up! You have won the battle."

A woman was struggling to make her marriage work without the primary support of her husband. He professed to be the breadwinner but allowed her to make the decisions although she had to give him the credit for the success. Her children did not know the true circumstance of the household or if they did, chose not to disclose their knowledge. Their mother dealt with the financial responsibilities without grumbling or complaining to others. She covered for their father's lack of giving to the household, including the children. They had no idea that the bills, the food, the clothing they wore, the holiday gifts for family and friends, the mortgage, their educational expenses, were exclusively a blessing from the mother who was favored by God. The praise they gave to their father, which he accepted, was a reward to their mother who set the stage for that to happen. Never once did the father ever acknowledge the mother for her virtue before the children. She cried for years in the night and smiled during the day, for she knew that victory would come in the morning. But she often wondered in her sadness–is anyone listening down here on earth to my heartache and pain? She wondered, but then, she got up and began another chapter in her life. What a loss! To live, to love and to provide but not to reside in the presence of loving people.

It is not enough to look to God for comfort. We need human hearts to provide intercessory prayer as well as encouragement. Individuals who nurture and believe in truth are the sources I seek when my days are darkest. God encircles my spirit and increases my enthusiasm for life when I, in my weakness, want to cry and relinquish the greatness that lies within. The trials of this world will take everything that is good from us unless we recognize that Christ is our stronghold. It is I who must stop crying and hiding from the truth. It is I who must listen first and allow the Holy Spirit to guide the way for others to hear my story and listen for the blessing that it brings.

The Scars Come Out At Night...

Have you ever noticed that when you are going through some rough times in your life no one seems to be up and around to watch with you the pain of your situation? Loneliness will come and darkness will appear even though the sun may be bright as the day.

You will look for family and friends and they will have excuses regarding their absence or failure to support. What I want to address is that period of time when you are left to yourself and what the night represents in your life. I have faced so many tragedies and heartaches that kept me up all times of the night. Most people who are going through a personal storm will tell you that the night time is not the right time to be alone. Usually misery and hurt comes to your bedside to disturb your peace and promise you few if any hours of sleep. Tossing and turning is another favorite treat during the night time of unrest. Getting up over and over again without reason is another reward. You contemplate calling those who have said to call them any time of the day or night but you've learned that most say those words to be kind.

Whatever you may have done wrong in your life will come out to haunt you in the night time. If you have hurt others and not been forgiven, don't worry, the night time will reveal your issues. Sleep becomes elusive and dreams come so prevalent that you question your sanity and existence. I visualize the night time inequities as my "scars" that won't heal until I have cleansed my soul and turned to God for deliverance. Saved or not, saint or sinner, you will receive a visit from your past. Scars can be a "victim" to your dreams and hopes for a successful future. You are in control of what happens in your tomorrow. Blame will alienate until you are left alone with bitterness as your companion. Listen, when God prepares a blessing for you, Satan will come in all of his perceived glory to tear you down and make you feel the least of all. Don't you know that what the enemy meant for evil–God meant for good? Don't you understand that where you walk, what you say and how you are blessed is sanctioned by God? Didn't you get the message in your suffering that faith and the Word of God will heal you no matter the condition?

Haven't you figured out that our Lord and Savior knows what the enemy has done to us and has Kept us under His protection? We have scars from wounds and hurts too numerous to mention and yet, we have a testimony. Cancer and disease couldn't take us out of the race. Broken limbs and broken hearts couldn't defeat us. Think about it, we got right back up and faced the problem. Persecution couldn't stop us–we shook hands with the enemy, and faith and hard work won them over. Rejection couldn't stand up to our love and ran off with hatred, jealousy and resentment. God knows what is best for us and He has provided for our return to normalcy. Satan cannot possess us, all he can do is upset us.

Girl, we have to get up from here and make it to our blessing. Nobody is going to give us what God has promised in His Word. We have to mobilize our efforts and reach up and out in order to manifest our rewards. Money alone will not help us but the love of God moving ahead of us will direct our path. Wait for me and if you don't, I have learned in the midnight hour of prayer to find my own way. I have been beaten down and traumatized for reasons not always of my own choice but I found a Savior. I found a reason to get up when I wanted to stay down. I found a friend who looked beyond my name and my situation and saw my need. Nobody can tell me about faith since I looked at myself in the darkness with no masks and no pretense. When I saw that my faith was weak and my life was at the brink of destruction, I found a friend. Night time is not the right time to be alone for you see things that frighten your well-laid plans. You hear things and you talk aloud to unseen ghosts in the night time. Past sins and things you thought were forgotten come to whisper in the night.

The interesting thing about the scars coming out at night is that you cannot run from you. You cannot hush the still, small voices within you. Whichever way you turn causes them to turn with you. Depending on where you are in your stage of personal development, you may be comforted or distressed by what you discern.

I learned in my night time forays with "my scars and the Holy Spirit" to trust God for my Word of comfort. I have a greater respect for the Holy Spirit now that I have been in the valley of despair. I have learned to appreciate the voice that whispers encouragement to me when I am ready to throw in the towel or who tells me the truth about me when I want to blame someone else. What a revelation to me! The scars remind me of what happened along the way to me and what makes me a whole person. I have experienced a combination of success and disappointments, heartaches and gain, trust and respect, suffering and healing, love and bitterness–but "it is all good" as the teenagers say because I have respect for the scars in my midnights.

Saying "Goodbye" Is a Choice!

"Is that my son? Is that my daughter? I am so glad to see you come home. Times are hard and crime is so rough that I worry when you leave the house. I'm glad you're home."

Well, Mom and Dad, I advise you to take a good look at your child because you may not see them leave and return in the manner that they left. You had better smile and rejoice with them while you can for tomorrow may never be theirs.

If you've got rules for your home and choices and consequences when they do wrong–you can keep your smile. If you know where they are and whom they represent–please continue to hold your peace. If you trust and gain respect in the process–you can keep your hope alive because it holds the future for your children. If you've got the power to mandate decisions in your household and control who comes in and who goes–you're a powerhouse in itself. If you can teach and preach and bind and find – you are responsible for your neighbor's child as well as your own.

The funeral homes are thriving and the jails are overcrowded with young men and women who act as though they created themselves. Who behave as though they have no parenting, no home and little, if any love. I want to know where are the parents?

When youth from 12-20 years of age can walk up to another and shoot them down without a cause or for a rumor–can you tell me, where are the parents? When the rights of others are neglected for fear from a few–will somebody, anybody, tell me who is raising who? When parents give up their rights as care givers, children become a major emphasis for all concerned. When inner-city dreams become rivers of blood and tears become the fountain – tell me, where are the parents?

When children gather in homes for club meetings and initiations to destroy one another, and nobody says "this house is off limits and so is my child," will somebody tell me where are the parents? When girls are raped while the videos are taped and family prayer has escaped, and no one seems to care, I wonder where are the parents? And when the police come knocking on the door, with the sad report, somebody always cries "Why did this happen? How could this happen? My child was a good child." And I say to you in times like these: Where were you when the same police asked parents in the neighborhood to support their efforts to decrease youth activities in criminal environments and you chose not to respond? Where were you when the truth was needed and you provided a false alibi and helped to create a menace to society?

We don't know what the future holds and that's why we as parents must prepare today for tomorrow and make every minute count. It's no use blaming others when we fail to do our part. Let's not wait for the concerns to escalate before we take action. We can start right now today, to take back our authority. If your child fails to obey and respect your leadership, provide other alternatives, apart from your other children who will "model" undesirable behavior. You've got to make a home worth the living, worth the challenges, worth the struggle to survive.

Don't stop love but don't be a co-dependent. If your child is under age, over age, and have no goals, to speak of, but they own "name brand every thing," get real. Stop pretending not to notice what is coming into your home or your child's life. What you don't see today may be your challenge tomorrow. Parents, you may have to give back the new car, refuse the new house, the mink coat, the clothes, the T.V. and VCR, that your "good child" bought with the dope money and be a soldier in the human rights army fighting for your family.

Smile, Mom and Dad because your children came home safe and sound but frown on their actions when others are not so fortunate at their expense. Don't say good-bye, say hello to new opportunities to make a difference in your home. One day your child will say "hello," to the greatest Mom and Dad in the world. You may hear them say. "Thank you for loving me enough to say no when my choices posed a threat to my goals and the rights of others. You valued and respected me when I wanted to live for the present but allowed me to see this precious day. A day some of my friends failed to see. My children will benefit from the teaching, the preaching, the leading, and the weeping that you gave to me." Saying good-bye really is a choice that we all have as a benefit of life.

THIS WORLD IS NOT MY HOME – I'M JUST PASSING THROUGH!
Sub Topic: Too Many!

As I prepared to speak to you today, I thought of many struggles that we have had to overcome in order to reach our career goals. I thought of the decisions made, good and bad, that shaped our character. I thought of opportunities for success–available to some and elusive for others. I came to bring you hope, tell you the truth, and encourage you that though we suffer many things in this life, we must remember that this world is not our home.

We are people joined together by hope. Chained together because of faith and crippled by the evils of slavery. Bound by determination and elevated by education. We are filled with religious principles and taunted by our own segregation by denomination. We are so often treated less than animals and yet yearning to be a master of his/her own life. We sing songs of salvation while recognizing that no one can save us but us. I came today to tell you that we've had <u>too many</u> troubles and not enough real successes–too many restrictions with too many predictions–There are too few marriages and far too many divorces. There are too many separations and not enough skills for self preservation. I want to stop, but there is too much black-on-black crime, and too many of us willing to settle for a dime. There is child abuse, wife abuse and too many of us saying "What's the use?"

In the innercity community there is too little hope and too much dope. Our streets are running over with tension and blood, while we laugh in theaters about 'Boyz in the Hood'. Too many parents are abdicating their rights to raise their children and the children are looking for nurturing in all the wrong places. Too many folks are wiping tears and waiting on an earthly savior to calm their fears. There are too many churches, on every corner, in too many cities, who are talking about a man named Jesus, who came to teach deliverance; and fail to leave the sanctuary long enough to reach out and touch lost souls, dying for the "real thing." There are too many preachers and missionaries who won't dare to preach that the members who pay more, save more, and find fault more, may be the reason the world will never truly know Christ in the truest sense of His mission. There are too many methods for dollars and too few programs for scholars. Too many remodeling projects to make the outward appearance of the building display a positive image and too few role models to make the inner sanctuary warm and welcome to members and visitors, not to mention living a spiritual life. In spite of these facts, we make it because we know that this material world is not our home.

Too many teachers are walking in classrooms and telling students that "I got mine and it doesn't matter whether you get yours"–too many good teachers are abused by the system because they expect students to learn, expect them to behave, and to leave the educational institutions ready for employment and a successful future rather than a street desire to "shuck and jive."–too many white people are believing in stereotypes and perpetuating a lack of opportunity for minorities, namely blacks–too many people have the power to make a difference and won't–not because a person is a minority or is defined as a quota, but because they are qualified to be promoted and recognized for the role they play in the organization–too many educated folks on the job have the audacity to say that we all have the same chance at success–too many are saying in this multi-cultural, diversified society, that "I don't see color"–Tell me this, why can't they see color when everywhere I turn there are people of color. At least be honest!

Too many blacks have made it "big" and have forgotten from whence they came. Perhaps, they have forgotten that the same people they pass on the way up may be the same resource they need on the elevator called "misfortune" that is going down–too many forget that they made it because somebody stood up, moved up, reached up, put up, and shut up to provide an opportunity for them to make it through the systems that are in power. They ought to be proud when they hear other folks say "Thank you" and "What shall I give?" Be proud because too many of them forget that those words represent resilience in the human vocabulary. Memberships don't make us, but they can break us. Job titles can change before you can cash your paycheck, but relationships can retire with you for a lifetime of memories. Start claiming your allies now for the war is at hand.

Too many teenagers with too many babies, by too many men, and too few opportunities. Girls, walking tall with pride, not understanding her lost opportunities–controlled by welfare, a form of slavery–chained by an unmotivated mind to rise above a bedroom mentality–too afraid to dream and bring that dream to life in the classroom and in the workroom–unwilling to become pro-active rather than reactive, while telling the "finest man in the world" that she is not for sale.

Too many babies are coming into the world by too young mothers who don't know what to do with them, about them, and for them. The "ooh's" and the "aah's" don't last long when the thrill of life is gone. Babies deserve a clean house, clean clothes, proper guidance and financial stability and those come after love and caring. Too many children are crying out for help while too many parents are walking away from the responsibilities that came much too soon. Too many children are eating peanut butter and jelly while the man in question eats the steak and tastes the cake.

Having a pretty baby means nothing when too many pretty babies are left in the garbage, on somebody's doorstep and at Grandma's house. What in the world is going on and what in God's name is going wrong when we ought to boldly stand up and tell young women, like my grandma used to say, "why should a man buy the cow when he can get the milk for free." I didn't say it–grandma did and she continued to speak her opinion until she died.

A woman has power to make a difference in her life, but she has to recognize it and assert that fact to those affecting her life. For example: A woman is like a bank account because she controls the deposits and withdrawals into her self-esteem account. She continually does a check and balance to see whether or not there are over drafts which impact on her well being. Her philosophy is "This is a joint account and it takes all of us, making regular deposits to create dividends for the future and I refuse to leave this world with less than I started with. I can do bad by myself."

She is a master teacher because she plans and implements her own lesson plans regarding the education of her family. Her credentials may not be acceptable at any level beyond her home, but she will gladly go on record supporting assertive discipline which may include corporal punishment. She's a self-taught woman!

Also known as a mother of this nation, she is a mover and a shaker wherever she goes because she can move and transport whatever she is designated to operate. She can carry one baby or a number of babies with or without assistance. This woman mobilizes her family and others to work while it is day because one day this earth will pass away. She reminds us that this world is not our home, we are only passing through.

She is representative of an Undertaker because she is not afraid to bury dead dreams and relationships when they get in the way if her positive goals. Her loved ones leave for the cemetery and each time she has to grieve and adjust for the welfare of those who depend upon her strength. She will undertake whatever she has to in order to endure the problems that exist in her life. And to top it off, she proclaims boldly that she is not troubled by the thought of dying.

A woman is a Surgeon, for she knows how to dissect the truth from fiction. She is a Lawyer because she understands that she is the judge and jury in any situation and no male can bring in a verdict that she has not agreed to participate in. She appears to be an Evangelist because she has morals and values that say "I don't need others to tell me to use condoms or birth control as long as I practice safe relationships according to the word of God."

She is like the Director of the license bureau because she tells the man of her life (one man) that she has a dog with a license, registered, with proper inoculations and no man can live with her under lesser restrictions. In other words, if she's worth having, she's worth marrying. A woman is a Policewoman because she can put a lock and key on her emotions and arrest the negatives that block her pathway. She represents the substance of gang membership in the highest order and needs no "hit man" to take care of her business. Too many folks know and respect her name, understand her game, for she makes it plain–that she works for what she gets and that's lesson #1!

Too many men are leaving their homes and families, looking at a figure they saw moving in slow motion. I guess they forget the songs, "Love the One You're With" and Don't Let the Green Grass Fool You." Too many sons are seeing their "fathers" give up on their wives and children and then, they too, learn to love them and leave them.

Too many young men have not learned to respect or value women. They call us obscene profane names as a put down, whether they call it stroking or rapping. Women are precious, but men have to be taught that to respect a woman is to love themselves. After all, we bring man into the world–that is if you want to get technical about the facts of life.

Young men need to see mature men 'weather' some storms and navigate to love and peace. They need to see fathers loving mothers and mothers loving fathers. Fathers need to be seen taking care of their responsibility, inside and outside the home.

I've learned that if I don't speak the truth, If I don't stand for something, I'll fall for too many ignorant stereotypes about my people. I don't know about you, but I'm tired of crying too many tears for my people who must continually fight for acceptance. I'm tired of too many family disputes and too many accusations that separate and divide us. I'm tired of too many fights and not enough victories.

In spite of too many things that happen, I'm happy for those who made it. Happy that one day a woman named Maggie Lee, who had a lot of black children, motivated me to be somebody. Out of her pain, rejection and many disappointments was a strong desire to live beyond today. My mother died, but her legacy runs deep and spans wide because of the message she shared with those around her. Society did not know my mother or my grandmother and they are both gone, but they believed in telling it to you straight, without a psychology book or any special techniques. They had too many rules, too many issues, too many hopes, or so we though at the time. I thank them now for the many words of wisdom, the love and the promises that "it would be all right." For always reminding us that we will never be alone. Never have to be afraid for our home has already been prepared beyond the cares of this world.

Yes, there is too much of everything and too little of the right thing. I can't speak for everyone, but I am thankful for the many individuals who live in the midst of drug environments and still remain "legally" drug free. I say legally because some people are addicts on prescription drugs and fail to understand the premise of "judge ye not."

I am grateful to many churches who realize that what's on the outside is far less valuable than the jewel on the inside. To the preachers and members who are more concerned with gaining through love and faith than by losing with criticism and indifference.

I salute, as all of you should, the many teachers who sacrifice their time, talent and finances to promote caring and diversity, regardless of race and religion–Teachers who may never wear a crown or receive the "Teacher of the Year Award"–The many teachers who hug the child with a hygiene problem along with the child who is clean and designer dressed–The teachers who encourage and build the esteem level of the failing student as well as the honor student.

It's time for us to celebrate the many single mothers and teenage mothers as well who believe in nurturing their children, instructing and disciplining them in the admonition of truth–Time for us to celebrate the mothers who deny themselves instant gratification for the love of their children–Women who tell prospective mates that my children and I come as a "package deal" and you cannot have one without the other–Time for us to celebrate the fact that no court can truly dictate to these parents how to develop or treat their children because family limits and rules are already in place and the parents are the head of the family jurisdiction.

We need to have pride in the knowledge that many fathers are not just biological fathers but they support the children that they father without being forced to by the courts. There are more than a few fathers who have custody of their children–Fathers who do not depend on relatives and others to share their responsibility–Fathers who love their wives and stay with their families throughout job losses, social humiliation and frustration. They make it work. They make it because love is not gender based, but reality based. After all, a real daddy looks beyond the "maybe's" and understands what it means to have babies.

I've been expecting too many miracles, for too many years, to accept less than the best. Too many folks standing in soup lines, and too many folks are homeless for far too many reasons. I can't understand it. I can't comprehend all the reasons why, but I believe that we will make it. We will because too many like Malcom and Martin, Fannie Lou Hamer and Rosa Parks, your mama and my mama, put their lives on the line to make our life choices more productive. Too many of us are looking back, falling down and saying foolish things like, "I will not be moved–I'm like a tree." However, we need to know that depending on the storm or the right equipment, trees can be moved. We need to be reminded that there may be too many statistics, too many problems, and too few answers, but never are there ever too many thanks for the works we have done.

As I close today, I have a request of each of you. When this event is over and anyone questions you about the message or the messenger, will you tell them that you met another drum major for justice in a little town, alive and well. One among many who support the premise that we are the driving forces for change. One who believes that Black folks are going to have to save Black folks because we are becoming the endangered species of the human race.

Remember that too many may seem like a lot and you can't take it, but hold on to your hopes because too many paved the way for you to get up and live. With unity and justification by our faith, we can plan to go home to peace, love and joy because our Father has prepared a place for us. Get your vision and look beyond the obvious and your deliverance will come. I see miracles and I am standing in line. Do you want to stand next to me?

Tribute to a Pastor's Wife

A pastor's wife must be strong in the Lord. She must believe that she can be all things to all people in spite of her treatment. She must be swift to ignore rumors which often surface in the church.

She must learn to cry on the inside and rejoice outwardly because there were no promises that her road would be easy.

If we were to ask for a wife's testimony, these are the words she might say:

"Being a pastor's wife is not easy. I've been one for a number of years and I know the thrill of victory and the agony of defeat. I'm not ashamed to tell you that it takes God in any home that spreads the gospel. There have been times when I've been neglected, rejected, suspected and disrespected, while my husband was praised and projected. Times when I had to smile in the face of adversity. Times when I wanted to cry but knew that I had to be strong for the sake of my mate, my children and my church.

Other women can wear what they choose, but I am constantly criticized and reminded that I am a pastor's wife. Evidently some people feel that I need to be reminded of my role but they fail to understand that I am first a woman. I need to be loved, appreciated, beautiful and notifed just as other women. I love nice clothes and a decent home with all rights and privileges that belong in a marriage.

When problems arise in the church and my husband is being discussed, I must gain strength from the knowledge that I am there to support him. If he is wrong, behind closed doors, I must communicate the truth of God's gospel and not mine. To be a minister is not to know everything but to relate to all things. I have to be wise as a prophet and gentle as a dove in order to love others in spite of what they do to me. So often accused, abused and misused while often amused and seldom excused, I hold my head up.

It hurts to see my loved ones hunger for acceptance. To see my husband walk the floor, praying for members and their families is painful to me. To see him shed tears for those faithful ones who grieve as well as those who die or are in trouble is so sad. But one day I know I shall stand before God and affirm my thanks for all he has done for me. Then I will ask to see once again my friend, my mate, my pastor, who has stood on the solid rock with me.

When we shall stand before the throne of Christ and hear Him tell our Father "These are they who have come up the rough side of the mountain. These are the ones who have washed their robes in the blood of the Lamb. Father, welcome them home." Then I shall hug my loved one and shout for joy throughout God's heaven. I have to tell Jesus all about our trials for He has never left me alone. "Yes." I've been a pastor's wife and "No," my living with this preacher man has not been in vain. I have not wasted my time, for up the road is eternal gain.

Dialysis Is Not My Master, It is My Testimony!

Several years ago, one of my younger sisters was diagnosed with Renal Failure and was a dialysis patient at a local clinic for three days a week. We were all devastated at what she had to endure prior to the illness and especially after the diagnosis.

I have never seen a person other than my mother take the news in such a calm manner. I knew that the physician had to do his job but this was news we dreaded for her to hear, although it meant that her physical condition would improve. Without the treatments she would not live. She sat up bravely while he spoke and silently digested the information. As an adult I have rarely seen her cry and she did not prove me wrong in this instance. We never saw her give up her struggle to survive. I saw the pain in her eyes and sometimes the unshed tears but not her resolve to use her kidneys again. The doctors were not optimistic. As a matter of fact, when I asked for information on her condition during the days of uncertainty about her recovery and care, the physician stated that she might have five years (a guess) to live. Wow! That was difficult for me to digest, although I did not share the information with my family or my sister at that time.

With no parents, although we have husbands, I was seen as the surrogate parent. I love my brothers and sisters so much that nothing is impossible when it comes to their well being. There was and still is no distance and resource issues when they call me in distress. At this point of our lives, this heartbreaking moment, we all felt so overwhelmed and so helpless, because we were unable to make it better for her in those days of suffering. I called our family and we prayed for her and stayed with her during countless visiting hours. No one in our immediate family had ever been on a dialysis machine to our knowledge. We knew absolutely zero about what this disease would entail.

My sister became more frail and seemed weaker and tired from the trips to the clinic. Her arms had knots from the implants and the needles. She began to complain about the caregivers and the rudeness of some of the physicians. The pain from the needles was increasingly uncomfortable to her and she was depressed from the medication and the feeling of being enslaved to a machine. It hurt to see her losing the vibrant, feisty spirit that I grew up with. Because I knew she was afraid and lonely at this new life change, I used to stop by the clinic and sit with her to keep her spirits up and to provide comfort. This experience in the dialysis world was new to me. There were people on machines and in the waiting room that I had not seen in a long time. To my surprise they were patients. I never suspected their illness when I saw them on the streets or in the church.

Everyone in the clinic appeared to know each other and the warmth they shared was encouraging to the onlookers. This world was cold and sterile to me.

Then I looked over at my sister who could not get used to this environment although medically she had no choice. I prayed with her and behind her back for her deliverance.

One day I talked to her and she was angry and hurt because she had seen insurance claims that indicated her life expectancy.

This was no silent woman who shared with me her conversation with the physician. She told him in no uncertain terms that she would overcome this disease and he had no business providing information to the insurance company that he had not shared with her. Allow me to paraphrase because I cannot remember all of the details and they are not necessarily important. What is important is what she did.

She proceeded to find her own donors without any fan fare.

In less than a year from the physician encounter, my sister had a donor. Her eldest son was a match. She did not receive much encouragement or support from the local physician but she found a kidney transplant specialist in Kalamazoo, Michigan who was wonderful. He agreed to do her transplant.

When the surgery was scheduled, most of us took the day off and we went to the hospital to support her and her son. It was a bleak, overcast day but for us the sun was shining. The inner light that brings hope and a sense of revival. We received quality service from the staff and the physicians before and after the surgeries. I was so proud and thankful for my nephew who gave above and beyond to save his mom. I was sure that if their roles were reversed, my sister would have done the same.

When they brought my sister and nephew out of recovery, we shed tears of joy. We knew that all was well because God is still in the healing business. I remember my sister saying to us that she saw our mother, when she awakened in the recovery room and that mom had "told her that it would be all right." I believed her and that gave me assurance that she would be whole and healthy for years to come. My sister is a living testimony of the power of God and faith that is difficult to explain.

She is back to work and doing well with a story to tell. Actually, she continued to work when she was a dialysis patient. Today as then, her clients know love and appreciation when they enter her line for employment benefits. Her smile and encouragement tell of her survival. Those who understand and wear the "suffering badge of courage" recognize the meaning of mastering the technology from the book of Grace. Thank God for blessing!

Define Parenting and Reap the Benefits

How wondrous! How precious are the parents who have given all they could to bring up their family in the admonition of God. Parents who have made tremendous sacrifices to deliver worthy and respectable citizens to a society that has been tainted by immorality and streets running with blood of innocent people. Parents who have stood on nothing but the promises of a Risen Savior to provide food, shelter, safety, and nurturing to the love of their lives.

So many parents deserve to be toasted and appreciated for being and not always doing. Maybe your recollections are not always positive because there are few saints on earth without some dirt on their wings. Since you are maturing, think on your desires and even your best, the mistakes that you have made. When economic times create hunger, stress, and neighborhood changes, the mature parents are the ones who create familial, communal opportunities for bonding and survival techniques. Name brand, may or may not, have been a household word, but your family name was a crucial reminder that you belonged to more than yourself. Mature, married parents raised children together and their decisions developed character and instilled principles of self worth and dedication. Single parents, who both carred and provided for their offspring, albeit in different homes, deserve to be blessed. Children never forget to give honor to whom honor is due.

Parents who live separately but support their children are the unsung heroes of families. Regardless of the circumstances surrounding the divorce, the illiterate status, the ugliness taht may have been involved in the relationship demise, these parents take responsibility for their actions. The children know that their father cares for them as well as their mothers or vice versa. The interesting change in the new millennium is the number of fathers who have total custody rearing males, females or both and they are committed and responsible. In some cases, more so than many of the mothers who are heads of households. Ideally, a family living together with children is our sign of excellence, guided by our spiritual knowledge God's plan for us, but this has not been embraced by the world. However, a parent in the house, without active leadership, participation and love is worst than having them present at all.

Foster parents and guardians are often the forgotten parents who provide nurturing and stability to so many children with special needs. Children who have been abandoned by parents with special needs. These are the parents who parent by choice, without adequate pay and praise, from those they serve. Their stars are on the sidewalk of time because they love unconditionally. Their reward come from the children who successfully make it in life and return to say "thank you."

Please don't forget the step parents who love despite testimonials and certificates of praise from either spouse or the children. Step parents who leave out the "step" in order to promote the "steps to building a foundation of respect and love without a price attached. Often they smile at the insult and cheer with the victorious, although it may be behind the scene. Those who are confident and have a true spiritual connection, reach for prayer when the going gets tough. They lean not on their own understanding but on the Word of God to guide them in providing what each child requires to be whole and healthy. They recognize that they are not biological but they are the one who accepted a role when they accepted their spouse. A badge of courage is extended when they look back and see the love returned that they provided from the heart.

A parent comes in many forms but the blessed parent is the parent who makes a difference without regard to the recipient. Children watch and model what they see. When the view is positive, what a wonderful enrichment for a parent to observe throughout their lifetime of maturity and growth. I am a parent and what a privilege to know that I am still growing and still sowing while I watch my harvest come in.

Can These Bones Live Again?

Of course they can! Though the bones be broken by the force of the circumstances, healing can fuse the bones together again and they will produce movement and strength.

Am I a bone to be discarded; buried and isolated? I defy anyone to say that these bones should give up and be defeated. We have only just begun to move with confidence and courage to do what must be done. A commitment was made to go to the poor and needy, to share encouragement with those in despair, and to provide resources necessary to build the kingdom of God.

These bones have substance that determines the individual's worth. A worth that does not devalue the human spirit despite the frailties of the human structure.

Folks tend to count you out of events and activities when the body has difficulty maneuvering from one point to another. Inactivity can cause insurmountable damage to one's system. When that occurs, the bones become brittle and weaken due to lack of exercise. It matters little, in reality, what others think–it is all about *you*.

Whatever has caused the regression in health, know that you can get up and live whole and healthy again. You can connect the bones together by eating, exercising and positive self-talk. What people say has no impact on your strong will and determination. I don't know about someone else's bones but I know that with faith and grace-these bones will live and prosper.

Chapter 5

Winning the Battle While Wrestling With Spiritual Demons

I See Dead People in the Land of the Living

In a land where prosperity is abundant and poverty is evident, we have a spiritual famine. I am not being sarcastic or pessimistic, I am a realist who learned how to tell the signs of the times by watching people. You learn in these creative years of wisdom to focus on what is presented and discern the truth, for it provides enlightenment to the soul.

I realize that this is deep in concept and perhaps I will be accused of morbid thinking. Maybe I will be labeled as a futurist who lived before my time or that I digested to many Vicodins or tranquilizers during my numerous bouts with health issues. On the other hand, a prophetess may suggest that I have undergone a series of spiritual "re-births" that have rendered me comatose until my umbilical cord has been severed from the world. If you are confused, imagine me trying to define why I am writing this. There is logic to my vision but you have to stay with me as it unfolds. The Holy Spirit is dictating and I am supplying the labor.

Recently I watched a movie called "Sixth Sense" about a boy who saw and talked with dead people. This movie has continued to stay on my mind. I often turn the channels of my television and lo, and behold, on previews, I see a young boy, sadly repeating the phrase to his mother "I see dead people." I began to think about those words and formed a spiritual connection between dead people and God's people. Also the fact that I truly know perceived dead people in this life, who circulate messages that are evident only to those who desire to spend time on the wild side. These individuals are willing to see beyond what society describes as normal and mentally rewarding experiences.

In my own psyche, I did not want to see the sadness, the death, the pain, the heartaches and the negative aspects of scene after scene of human misery. I suppose it reminded me of my own life story of pain and suffering. The message slowly gained momentum that this town I live in has so many memories of those I love embodied in my mind, those in the cemetery and remembered faces in my photo albums. Drugs and alcohol have rendered so many people incapable of a rational decision and caused unbelievable heartache to undeserving parents, spouses and children.

What in the world is going on and what is going wrong? When babies are having babies and think they have all of life's answers–my question is answered. When gay life styles are okay to everyone but those who profess it–something is wrong. When churches are too busy trying to entertain and maintain a numbers game rather than save the dead among them and on the streets of Gomorra–tell me who are the living? When children prefer gang life over prayer life, a war is created and guess who appears to be winning?

When parents are abdicating their parental rights to be a friend rather than a parent in control–where is the victory celebration for future success? When money becomes the end all and the body becomes the show all–watch for the payoff. It appears that dead people are increasing but so is the prophecy that God will not forsake us or leave us. He knows what is best for each of us and we hold the key to our purpose. I asked a question of church members: Is anybody real? Through examples and meaningful dialogue, the response was that he is real but man is weak. Therefore, as weak individuals, we must be constantly reminded that we are not our own but children of God, who require direction and discipline.

What is the definition of a dead person in the land of the living? According to the dictionary, a person is considered dead when "deprived of life; lacking power to move i.e. sealed or responded; numb; incapable of being stirred emotionally or intellectually. It is the time of greatest quiet; no longer in use; lacking power or effect."

People are alive physically without goals and the ability to effect change in their lives. The desire to make creative decisions other than for the moment are non-existent. Without the power to motivate and elevate one's mind to a higher level, there is no success. To be stirred emotionally and intellectually, a person must embrace life and see hope in the darkest moment of their situation. To give up when the odds are against you is the depth of sadness especially for a vibrant spirit who profess to know a living God. Faith without power is like a Shepherd without a flock. Faith with power is power energized and satisfied by the Holy Spirit, ordered by Jesus and approved by God.

I wish people would examine their claims of seeing horrible visions and apparitions while at the same time testifying to believers that God can do anything but fail. When a vision comes, we ought to turn to the Word of God for understanding and revelation because there is a purpose to everything that happens. All visions should not be of dead people or tragic events. There ought to be some joy, some peace, some love and some prosperity in our sight.

Of course, I see dead people in the land of the living. I see them in my family and your family. I see them in the church, sitting like a victim in the pew. I see them in the school yards, behaving like the man possessed with demons. I see them in homes with hungry looks and no parent in sight. I see them with children, in despair and with no job. I see them in the streets, fighting like fools, with no rules and no schools. I see them complaining about the government and economics but they refuse to vote or stand up and be counted. Oh yes, I see dead people in a land of the living and I cry in advance of an obituary because I know that "except for the grace of God, there go I."

There is hope for us. There is a role for us to play. We are powerful and with faith all things are possible. We are not deprived of life. We have the answer and the resources to help the dead be revived. We do not lack power. We are tired but with quiet and sleep, we will rise again, whole and healthy. Emotionally and intellectually, we are capable of "stirring up the gift within us" to make a difference in our lives as well as others. As long as we see dead people, we have a job to do as Christians but if we, too, become dead people, the world will do a job on us. I don't see dead people as often as I used to because I choose to see living people ready for a Word from the Master so they can take up their "bed (circumstance in life) and walk."

Faith When The Odds Are Against You!

Now faith is the substance of things hoped for, the evidence of things not seen. Hebrews 11:1. Be confident in you because "you" have all you need to make it through the burdens of this world. God has a calling on your life and you are anxious to go forward. Without faith you cannot please God. Without the Holy Spirit, you will not be sure of your purpose.

Sometimes you go through so much mess, you don't know who in the world you are but you hold on to the promises of your Deliverer. You create so much stress trying to please everybody but yourself.

Yesterday you thought you would not make it, then you were reminded of a word, a phrase that you learned as a child. Words that inspired hope such as "In all these things we are more than conquerors through him who loved us." Romans 8:37

You will know Satan when he comes against you because he will confuse you and cause disorder in your life. Peace and joy will become elusive. Every time you settle one situation, another will go astray. Faith will become more and more important because without it, you cannot stand.

You care about those you inadvertently hurt since faith took hold of your mind and shook you back to reality. Why give up what you have worked so hard to accomplish?

I remember so many people who gave me strength and determination. They instilled many values and ethical principles into my home training. I do not claim to have appreciated at that time all that was shared with me but I learned and I grew and I thank them now for the knowledge. It is up to you to remember your heritage and cultural background as you seek for ways to overcome the odds against you. The people of this world could care less whether or not you make it to your success. You are the motivator, the numerator and the common denominator. I had to continually reach down to support others and then look up repeatedly to see hope for my self.

There will always be odds working against you in many areas of your life but God specializes in cases such as these. While you are trying to "figure it out-God is already working it out." When your miracle, your blessing, your reward, is knocking on the door for entrance, the odds will elbow its way in to block your delivery. What do you do? Do you give up? No, of course not! You act like touch football and surround yourself with key defense players who will help you to win and head for the goal line. You may get battered but that is a part of this game called life. All you have to remember is who is calling the shots; who has the power and strength to carry the ball to the finish line. I don't gamble but I see faith making a touch down.

I'm Crying-Who Is Listening?

Lord, give me strength when the adversity is knocking at my door. I need strength when my very presence invites controversy and negative speculation. I am crying on the inside but my mask of smiles conceal the turmoil from those who know me. I learned from the past to hide my pain in order to gain God's character building reward of self love. What I am relearning is that hiding my pain is not the solution, acknowledging it and activating my faith is.

Sacrificing my self worth was never an option. It seemed, at times, that no one cared whether my needs were met or not. I realize that the blame lies entirely with me but I wonder if I can get someone to admit partial responsibility for my emotional distress. Before anyone questions my sanity, please understand that no one can affect my well being unless I allow them to. I did not allow my spiritual side to move fast enough to evade the human weakness that rushes in to overtake me at my lowest point. My defeat is operating from that element if I do not focus on my hopes and goals for the future. Today I am affirming to myself that the tears must cease and my joys must increase. I will not get my blessings while I worry about others and their perception of me. Whatever my fears, whatever my heartaches, no one caused them but my own idiosyncrasies.

I have cried for so long "why me," that I can hardly breathe the words out loud. And then I tell myself that "a woman like me can take the pain of a situation and run with pride knowing that I am all that and more." Folks who discuss my shortcomings and use the rumors they hear to limit my success evidently don't know that I am a powerhouse of victorious energy. I refuse to cringe, avoid, and ignore the experiences that I have overcome. I refuse to walk around folks who dare to question my abilities and my qualifications as a professional. I don't require affirmations for myself as an individual. I mandate love and principles of trust and mutual respect.

Everything I have gone through has prepared me for future growth and prosperity. If the unbelievers would search the biblical verse of "To whom much is given, much is required," they would understand that I don't have time for trite remarks and unethical motives. I have been blessed abundantly and all that I have been given must be shared for the cycle to continue. When others are resting on their laurels, I must be about my Father's business.

Maybe the tears have come, unbidden and unforeseen, down my cheeks but now I celebrate the support that is available when they show up. It is apparent to me that someone, somewhere is listening as I softly go to the cross and empty my cup.

HALO OF DEPRESSION

This depression has sapped my strength,
Strangled my will and made me feel
As though I have no will.
It makes me frown when I'm down to the ground.
"Depression, why do you insist on persecuting me?
Say the word and I'll set you free
For you are not what you claim to be."

You make me cry when I want to be happy.
You keep sadness lurking, always near,
When I cannot see through darkness and fear,

You are the one to bring the fog and the gloom.
But in my life there's no room,
For rainy skies and tear stained eyes–
For mournful lies and grim replies.

Leave me now, where there's no despair–
Nor a harsh word to mar my view,
For I deserve peace of mind without a care.
Dare I trust this feeling so long my due?

Of course! I must take each day with it's ups and downs,
And tell depression to leave me barren as I face the sun and it's direction.

Eulogy of the Devil

My brothers and sisters, I come to you today with happiness and no regrets at the passing of our adversary, the devil. He has been applauded by many, and scorned by others and yet, he prevailed.

As Christians cried–he laughed–as sinners sought a refuge–he kept the warfare alive in order to keep them in bondage. Sickness plundered homes and encouraged death to come forward at his command. Trouble appeared from every corner of the world because he was known as the "dark prince, unafraid to take on God's strongest warriors." It was so sad that he was unable to delight in the Lord Jesus Christ, our Savior. Unfortunately for him, the light of the world was an abomination to him. Light and darkness cannot dwell in the same place, at the same time. God will not dwell in an unclean temple.

The devil was called by many names. He was identified as the "adversary," the "old serpent, "the "enemy," "wicked," "a murderer," "liar," "Satan," "a Thief," "Mammon," "Accuser of brethren," and "demon," "the devourer," among others. Through his persuasion, so many saints were tempted and destroyed by the power of sin. He robbed them of their eternal residence in heaven. According to him, he never made anyone do anything against their will. The choice was theirs to make. What more can we say about this peace breaker, this untrustworthy leader of cults?

He excited us with temptation because he knew what we wanted in our lives. It was so difficult to stand with strength when you placed your mind on forbidden fruit. Satan knew how to sow and develop the fruit to deceive the very elect and we fell for it. He failed to tell us that the tempter's wrappings were artificial and what you saw was not always what you got. In other words, he told us that "we should have known better than to let the green grass fool us." He convinced some saints to desire alcohol and drugs so much that they would kill their dreams and their loved ones in order to sniff, drink, inject, and free-base themselves to death.

Let's face it. The enemy had power. He was extremely knowledgeable about our business, our goals, and our beliefs. Our major weakness was that we never really knew him. Some of us believed fairy tales about a red suit, forked tail, and horns. How sad for this deceiver. He rejoiced in our ignorance of him because he never missed a soul that believed the stereotypes and myths. Folks who refused to study, who failed to attend Bible Class, Church School, Sabbath services, nor accepted the work of God were prime candidates for his mission.

He created hatred among the brethren as well as those in the world. He made sure that loving folks began to speak unkind words to those who praised and loved them. They became envious of the success of others and jealousy caused them to become bitter. This devil, spurned from the depth of darkness, shouted with joy as we became liars and truth became our enemy. He had a "special glow" when we testified in church about loving everybody for he knew every hypocrite in the congregation. He loved to stand back and watch the conflict that developed when the truth was revealed. His power was awesome (or so it seemed), as he hired and fired as though he paid the cost to be the boss. He always neglected to tell us that God was truly in charge.

In the book of James, Chapter four, to be exact, the seventh verse, the Apostle Paul is saying "resist the devil and he will flee from you." When we didn't resist, he challenged us with words like these, "I double dare you to run from what you know you can't resist." How dare he challenge a child of God who made it through storms and tribulation to get to this moment in time? He forgot who this child belonged to that he was messing with–an anointed, Holy Ghost inspired–Saint of God. These were Saints who had stood the test of time–who came up the rough side of the mountain–who had washed their robe in the blood of the lamb–who knew healing from sickness–comforting in sorrow–pleasure in pain–and security in a storm. Time saw him at work and reported to God, so that he would manifest himself.

The devil loved to test Saints. Remember Job–the devil took everything physical and material from him but could not shake his faith. Job vowed, "Thou you slay me, yet will I trust Him." Remember how the devil made a liar out of Abraham and an unbeliever of his wife Sarah but they stood on the Word of Lord in the end and were granted favor? He tried Jesus in so many ways and failed because Jesus, the Creator, knows all there is to know about the wiles of the devil and his deceitful practice toward Christians.

There were many who felt the stain of sin, the infirmities and the heartaches caused by the deceiver. Ask Moses, the prophet of God, who thought it better to suffer for the promised Christ than to own all the treasures of Egypt. Ask Rahab, the prostitute, how faith in God can deliver you when the enemy has you surrounded.

What more can we say in this hour of truth? Shall we lie as we often do when a life has ended its journey? Shall we sing praises to this dark prince of evil and darkness? No, we will tell the truth and be free and blessed for an occasion such as this–a home going celebration for the devil. Be very sure as you view his remains that your anchor holds and grips the solid rock of faith because he still has the power to rise again. It is up to you to defeat him with the power of the Holy Spirit. Build a fence around you and your family through prayer and supplication and watch the Word become a living, vibrant being.

This devil has many relatives to mourn his passing. He leaves a host of disturbed minds, friends, trouble makers, peace breakers, gamblers, adulterers, drug abusers, liars, thieves, and other reprobates. Numerous other relatives and unbelievers preceded him in death.

After the funeral services and burial, we will greet you in that city of darkness and destruction to await resurrection day. Further instructions will follow based on personal testimonies of faith and witnesses.

I See A Light–Is That My Breakthrough?

"All right girl, you can lay down if you want to but there must be a way out of no way. Hang your head if you want to but I see something that the natural eye cannot see–a blessing coming to me, for me."

When you are going through a storm, every day seems like a perpetual cloud that will not allow the sun to shine. Attempts to smile and look beyond the situation take your limited strength to the depth of despair. Emotionally you are drained. You pray for relief and release. Tears hover below the surface and wait for the critical moment of pain and hurt to overflow.

You look at others who live lives of shame and degradation but do not see their sad state of affairs. They are rarely sick and are prospering financially. Doors open to them on all sides and they receive love and appreciation though they scheme against the righteous. You wonder when a light will shine at the end of the tunnel for you.

"Where is it" you whisper, "where is my break through? God is my source, my health and my strength and I am in the dark without an anchor. I have faith. I have belief in Christ as my savior but my ship has not docked and my inheritance is missing. I know that heaven has a seat for me and treasures beyond my imagination.

I also know that my father in heaven has wondrous blessings for me down here in earth. Some things have been stolen from us by Satan and we have to take them back. I don't mean like a fool going into a bank demanding that they turn over the keys to us because it all belongs to us. But be a fool for Christ, with a belief in the promise that tell us to ask anything in his mighty name and know that we can have it.

You have to trust God even if you do not see a sign. You have been there in that place and time where hope is in short supply and victory is in your dreams. You have cried for days on end until you learned how to reap the benefits of sowing a well-planted harvest.

I know that you want to put your head in the air and tell everybody not on your "Wave length" to move on up a little higher. Your tolerance for negative talk and selfish behavior is very low. You are on the verge of a nervous breakdown with fading thoughts of your breakthrough. Just when you think you've had enough and the storm is ready to overtake you–a light appears. It shines so bright that you are able to see resources, real and hoped for, emerge as a reality. For the first time in years, a clear and focused view is clear for your eyes alone. You can have what you say.

The impossible seems so close that you can reach out and touch it. Your victory is in holding fast to the present and expecting the best of the future. There is no turning back. The people, the things, the circumstances, that crippled your abundance investment cannot harm what God has placed on your table of blessings. They have tried in unbelievable ways to block you but you stood, strong and invincible, with faith as your shield. Look at you, girl. You are ready for your break through when others thought you were out of the race.

You know without a doubt that the light is for you. You know it because the Word has told you it was coming if you faint not. Yes, you will see a light and it will be your break through. When it is your time, you will know it for the light will only shine on you.

Lord, I Give My Life To You!

Lord, I give my life to you. You are my friend and Savior that I worship through good times and bad times, I praise your name. Without you, I am nothing, but with you, I can do all things.

I know that you are interceding on my behalf in every area of my life; financially, spiritually, emotionally, mentally, socially, professionally, psychologically. You can do anything. I have what I asked for because you, have answered my prayers so many times and delivered me from adversity.

I have been in darkness and brought into the marvelous light. Because of jealously and envy, my light was hidden and I was left to find God's will on my own. I witness to others of the mighty God that we serve who allows our light to shine and how he took me from obscurity and brought me into the presence of the anointed. I had to come forth, prepared through his word to speak to men and women of the risen Savior. A Savior who pushed me through the womb of life and allowed me to give birth to myself.

I am healed by the redemptive blood of Jesus. Few can understand why I cry with joy, shout with unashamed praise, and testify anywhere, but they don't know that I've given God what he gave me–love and praise. He threw in forgiveness and hope with joy and peace as a chaser. I am drinking in the blessings of his Word. "Lord, I have stood on your Word. My life belongs to you unconditionally. I have given my life to you and now I wait for the abundant fruits of the spirit to come forward. I freely give my life to you and it is all about mutual love an respect."

I Am A Selfish Friend–Don't Leave Me Alone…

"We are so sorry, we've done all that we can do. We'll make her comfortable and send her home to be with family and friends." Those words are etched in my memory, not once or twice, but a number of times. Another friend whom I dearly love gone to be with the Lord. The pain and agony of loss is too great for me to describe. I will discuss one friend and her loss because until you lose a close friend, no one can tell you about the empty space that is left in your heart.

How could a woman, so beautiful, gifted, and talented, my best friend for many years, die so young? How could a merciful God reach down and take, of all his creations–my best friend? My wonderful, kind and loving friend who knew my ugliest and most precious secrets. She knew my sinful passions and joyous pleasures for we could share so much. We knew each other better than our mates could comprehend especially when our menopausal events began. I remember when she found out that her marriage had an "uninvited guest." A guest who almost destroyed what most people consider a "model home." I took her cue and smiled as people complemented her on her "fine and loyal" husband. She lived through ther drama and played her part well.

When her children grew up and rebelled against the family rules, we prayed together and cried together, not always in that order. When they got their lesson in the school of hard knocks, we both sighed in unison as they confessed their faults and gave their lives to Christ.

As the economic climate changed, she lost her job and hubby terrific refused to give her money for items beyond the basics. I took my few dollars and we made it through the poverty stage. After all, that is what friend's are for. Most of all, we didn't talk about loans or "so much on a dollar." If you are ethnically inclined, you will know what I mean. We were not selfish with each another. We felt the privilege of friendship and now she is leaving me in this cold, unfriendly world. And the sad thing is I have no power to stop her. I have prayer on my knees, standing up, sitting down and lying prostrate on the floor. I have begged God and pleaded with him to heal her pain-ridden body and I think he has forgotten me. "Forgive me Lord. I know better but my heart hurts so bad. I am emotionally and physically drained. If it is your will, please let this cup pass from her." Evidently the answer was no because she is steadily slipping away.

I watch her face and glazed though her eyes are, she searches for my face. We both understand the diagnosis and the eventual prognosis. You see, we thoroughly researched the library for reference material regarding this disease. What we feared is now a reality. No one must know the truth until she is ready, other than her mate. As a matter of fact, He does not know that I am aware of the situation although the knowledge helps me to comfort him as well as the children. I watch them cry and I think to myself "they don't deserve this sorrow and neither do I."

The code blue signal begins and her eyes are closed in death. I am selfish because all of a sudden, I feel so alone though the room is filled with family and friends. There is still so much that I want to tell you but there is no more time. Who will I turn to when the trials are many and the days are lonely? Then I hear a small voice within that whisper to me "let go and allow her to make her journey in peace. You were the greatest gift she could ever shop for and the best friend she could ever hope for. Cry and get up and help celebrate her passing to a better life."

Everyone is leaving and I must have a few moments to talk with her spirit as I gaze at her physical body. "Good-bye, my friend of so many years and a barrel of tears. How can I really be alone when you left me with so many memories of true friendship? Will you smile through my cloudy days and pause to say "hello" during some of life's many storms? Didn't we have some good times? When my mate is "working on my last chocolate nerve," who will rescue me and take me out to eat somewhere in the neighborhood like you always did? Those times accounted for our voluptuous-physical presence. You remember how we used to come up with all kinds of kung fu moves and choke-holds to use on our male counterparts when we were angry? You assured me that you would hold him while I implemented the domestic violence. Our laughter would ease the tension because we knew that we were not equipped nor prepared for the task.

It is so hard to say "good-bye" to you when we rarely said the words. We would wave or say "see you later, love you" and never thought about one of us not being here. We had good times and bad times but the good news is that I will see you again. I've already made my reservation and I will search heaven over until I find you. We will walk the streets of glory singing Zion songs. People standing around think this is all to it but you and I know better. I promise I will continue to set the goals and plans we discussed for my future prosperity. I will cry, over and over again, and then–I will get up and live. If I don't get up, my love and friendship was in vain.

Your children will know love from a surrogate mother and your mate will be remembered. I will keep the women from kidnapping your mate after you are gone, for a period of time, as though I can smile.

You never could sing a tune on key but when you join the heavenly choir, will you try 'What a Friend We Have in Jesus?' Since I can't sing either, I'll volunteer in my choir to sing the same song and I promise that we will be in harmony. Sleep well, my friend, and I will see you in the morning."

My Tongue Has a Sweet Savor!

Life and death are in the tongue. Release the power of your words and watch God work miracles. God has the ultimate claim over our lives and he can do anything but fail. I have the faith but God has the power. When I am weak, He is strong. I will make it because "greater is he that is in me than he who is in the world." I now understand that I cannot claim anything that is a blessing to me until I learn to control my tongue and unleash the greatness that lies within.

I am a powerhouse that sits on a hill in my community which will not be hid. There is a light that shines through me that warms those who come near the flame buried deep inside of my soul. People cling to my words wanting to hear more from a chosen vessel of God, wounded and healed of my transgressions but washed in the blood of a forgiving Savior. No one can surmise what has brought me to this moment, to this time in my life. I am eternally grateful for what my Father in Heaven has done for me. I am thankful for what he continues to do.

Without outward praise to others, without energy and enthusiasm for his promises, without a testimony to his healing and deliverance, without a witness to his love–how can we tell the world about this living, breathing God? A God who brought us all the way from poverty to victory. One who brought us from shame and blame to abundance and a new name, from sorrow to a healed spirit. What a mighty God we serve!

I am better today because he lives. His miracle-working power elevated me in the presence of mine enemies. He gave me prosperity when I literally came through fire and devastation. When I think about all that he has done for me, I cannot help but praise his name. "I look to the hills whence comes my help, knowing that it comes from the Lord" and my faith begins to rest on God's promises. I have to act on what I desire through prayer and verbally speaking my request.

We are in a fight, a struggle for our very existence. We must stand though the enemy surrounds us on all sides. We've got to stand even though life storms are raging–stand up, my sister, though our homes are leaning from an assault of the enemy. We can do it. We are strong enough to do anything. We can tell that deceitful adversary where to go, how to go and what his schedule will be. Don't be afraid!

Remember that with God on our side, there is no mountain high enough to keep us from our goal. We can tell the devil "to get out of our way" with the authority of God. He told us in Isaiah 54:17 that "No weapon formed against us shall prosper: And every tongue that rises against thee in judgement thou shalt condemn. This is the heritage of the servants of the Lord and their righteousness is of me."

So then, my sister, our tongue has the propensity to bless or curse us, kill us or revive, and I am in agreement with you that we live to gain rather than lose in this game called life. We are a royal family of believers who know what power we possess. If we are not ashamed of the Father, He will not be ashamed of us. After these things are reaffirmed, we can claim with our mouth those things that we ask in the name of Jesus Christ of Nazareth.

I Met Jesus At the Pool of Saloam!

I felt the Master's presence at the hour of my greatest need. Now I can share with others that I have been with him for a certainty. God was with me because I felt his presence. I was surrounded by warmth, love and comfort. I cannot explain every emotion I experienced but my fear was removed.

Doctor Jesus met me at my lowest point. I wanted to give up and quit this race of failure and defeat. This was a time when my rejection, my infirmity was most acute. I felt the least of all. He spoke peace to me–actually called my name. He gave me the authority to command my healing and peace of mind to be as though it were. He gave me the right to claim my inheritance without lies and scheming.

He demonstrated his love for me in spite of my unbelief. He did not force me to accept his Words or his healing. He prepared the way and I walked therein. A mission of service began within, down in the deep recesses of my mind, captivated my heart, motivated my spirit and I began to rise. Because I had been ignored, knocked down, accused and abused, so many times, I felt that I could not move. My mind refused to stop looking back to the past attempts to get up and I had to press, press and push my way to hear and see my Savior. You don't understand why I believe he had to be my Savior. I knew that no one else would give me all rights and privileges to see the full measure of his promises.

I had to know without a doubt that God wanted me to have the best of health. He wanted me to have abundance here on this earth. His Word told me to thank Him for the little things and the big things, but praise Him for what He is going to do. God won't move until I am ready to have Him trouble the healing waters that are meant to bless me.

I felt the stirring of something inside of me and I whispered "what is this? This thing that won't allow me to step to my success, to my healing, to my prosperity, to my joy–what is it?" The whisper turned to a shout of confirmation and I put my mouth and my limbs in the hands of the Master. I knew that this time I would make it. God has done so much for me. He made the enemy leave me alone. He protected me while I was lying at the pool of my Saloam, unable to move, and yet He loved me enough to stop and talk to me. Since He came, my life is no longer the same.

Now I don't wait to be told to get up and walk, I get up running because I know who it is that knocked at the door of my heart. I know who cared enough to tell me the truth in order to help me make it. I know the source of my salvation. When you see me, you will see a woman who represents change. You will see a woman who met Jesus and invited Him to stay and minister to her while she freely swims and bathes in the healing waters of Saloam.

Encouragement Is Like a Letter...

Hello My Friend:

This letter is a long time coming. Please forgive me for not obeying the Holy Spirit earlier. As Mother's Day approaches, I was inspired to let you know what a beautiful and anointed person you are. You care about those you love as well as others around you. God blesses when His witnesses reach out to comfort and encourage.

Your smile touches more than you know. It warms and brightens up the sad and lonely spirits you meet and greet every day. When your good intentions are evil spoken and your love is rejected–hold fast to the Word of God. He promised "never to leave you or forsake you."

I think of you when I think of myself and the losses I have suffered. We have so much in common. I have cried in my midnights and looked high and low for my "hi-lights" and yet, I still believe that there is a Savior who can deliver me. His name is Jesus Christ and our soul is His to claim. I often see tears in your eyes, though they don't fall down. Behind your smile, I sense hurt so deep, sometimes, that you don't raise your head. I am sure the enemy has attempted to take your life and that of those around you. The devil doesn't care what he has stolen from us–he only wants to see us defeated. It is our job to take back what he steals from us.

You have shown that you are a survivor, a witness, a refuge and a friend. God has a blessing, many blessings in store for you. Continue to love and trust Him for all of your needs and He has promised to supply them.

Hold your head up and know that you are not alone. Christ is near and I am here to answer your call. Make your requests known to Him and watch Him deliver on time.

I value our friendship and the love we share. Dark though our days have been, we have witnessed sunshine and joy beyond compare. I feel the fire of the Holy Spirit burn within my soul and I know beyond a doubt that Christ lives inside this temple of mine. Dream and then plant your seeds of faith and watch the harvest of your blessings. You have made your deposits–now make your withdrawals while the interest is high.

Remember that you are not alone in the twilight of your years. You are crossing through time in route to your destination (heaven) which the travel agent (minister) has shared with you so many times. The ticket master (Jesus) is standing at the gate waiting for you to board and He knows whether you have paid the price to ride this train. We can enjoy blessings right here on earth as we prepare for our journey. In the meantime, we have each other and most of all, we have the Lord.

Lovingly,
Your Friend In Christ

You've Been Down Too Long!

Your situation has been sad and pitiful. Perceptions of your friends and family have caused you to falter. The mean things said about you and to you have hurt too deep for you to respond. Those you have opened doors for are the ones who close windows of opportunity for your success. I feel your pain but you've been down too long.

It is time for you to rise and walk without fear to your inheritance. The prosperity and abundance promised to you in the Word of God are available to you. "Don't be weary in well doing, for you shall reap in due season, if you faint not" (Galatians 6:9). God never told us that we would not suffer and He assured us that He would "never leave us or forsake us."

I've seen you with your head down and a million, or so it seemed, frowns on your face. There were so many times that I wanted to comfort you but your pride spoke loud and clear "I can do this by myself. I can overcome what just happened to me. Please ignore me and pretend as I am doing that everything is all right." I turn away, as do others, because we know that one day your strength will come. You have been down too long and it's time to remember who you are. It is time for you to listen to your inner voices of self confidence which will influence your decisions. It is time for you to develop your vision statements as well as create a vision of what you want to become. Recognize that age is not a factor in developing your vision statement. If you can see it you can be it. There will always be naysayers who doubt your vision and goals, but when they show up, show them an anointed believer of miracles. You don't have to be pompous or boastful but allow them to know the source of your contentment.

What you fail to realize is that all you have been through has prepared you for this journey of retribution and restoration. The enemy comes to "steal, kill, and destroy." You must not allow him to steal your joys, your hopes, and your dreams. When he kills the depth of your spirit, you no longer exist as an individual of purpose. The Holy Spirit has done everything except send smoke signals to get your attention. Every weapon that has been fired at you by the enemy lowers you to the standards of the adversary. May I give you some advice from my pages of desolation before my consecration? A child of God, anointed and directed by the power of the Holy Spirit will always be a target; an enemy of our adversary, Satan. With your head down and defeat across your demeanor, you invite constant attacks.

Do not look for favor from anyone other than the Master because He can deliver what the world only talks about. Begin to smile more readily, even though what you hear is upsetting you and tearing you apart on the inside. This world calls this behavior "kissing up" or "brown nosing." I remind people who know me that I have a brown nose anyway, therefore, I am keeping it real. I call it survival and spiritual. The more you smile, the more God allows you to rejoice. Feeling sorry for yourself is human nature but few people can stay down for long without difficulty in standing, strong and focused. You need to be up in order to know what lies ahead of you.

What God had for you is already on the way to your address. It has been blessed and labelled with your name on it. It has love and respect stamped on it. It has been sealed with a hug and marked "fragile handle with care." God has angels on duty, ready to wipe your tears, when your distress signal goes off. Remember the times that you thought you could not make it but somehow you did. The "somehow" was angels who were raising up a standard against satan for your renewal and your revival.

I want you to sow a seed and reap a harvest. "Ye have not because ye ask not" (James 4:2). I want you to receive all that belongs to you by boldly standing on the promises of God. I want you to make it, to believe the impossible, and make a change in your circumstances. Get up from where you are and expect your blessings. They are enroute to you from everywhere: your enemies, your past relationships, defunct jobs, disobedient children, recent associations, just to name a few. God is trying to restore to you what the devil has stolen from you. The enemy cannot destroy your vision or take your soul for they belong to God. Get up, my friend, for you have been down too long. I want to rejoice with you but you must be in control of your own spirit, mind, and body in order to collect on God's promises. You are the only one who can sign for the blessings being delivered to you. If you spend your time down instead of standing up, answering the door of opportunity, what can you say? God has something better for you and with a vision of faith and determination, you can have what you say.

You Can Be a Christian and Talk About Love Between a Woman & A Man!

Christian people feel uncomfortable talking about love between a man and a woman. But they hurry to criticize the results of what the term "illicit relationships between the two means."

God made both male and female and intended for them to love each other. Not just to love on a sunny day but for better or worse. It is easy to love on sunny days, for those are the fun, the sexually active, the smiles, the "why me worry" days. It's easy to love when the figure is ripe for the power control is usually in the male court. The hair is "usually vibrant and the gray is absent." It's a sunny day when arthritis is heard about, and sugar is in the box on the table.

It's time to talk about this love thing because it's a real issue that's coming up in conversations daily. The better or worse may come in the form of illness, joblessness, spiritual weakness, financial struggles, infidelity, mental pressures, inability to have children, and loss of attractiveness. These are only a few. Inspite of these barriers, Christians have to hold on and know that somebody is still in love, praying and trusting in God, regardless of the obstacles.

The church has lonely women and men inside its walls. Single women especially, who come to church, in some cases, as a substitute for a meaningful, action-filled life. I realize that this statement may invoke some disagreement but the facts have been self evident. I once polled a number of women (privately) regarding this issue and they agreed with my hypothesis. According to those interviewed, the moment the relationship with a prospective mate became serious, the church relationship changed. Usually their attendance began to lag or became non-existent. They had difficulty determining why the change occurred or when it actually began.

There are married women in the church who are lonely for a number of reasons. They may be lonely even if their mates attend church on a regular basis or hold some major position of authority in the church. Logic requires that time and attention be a provision of nourishment for marriage vows and if this does not occur, problems will surface in the relationship. The worst relationship is the lonely, married woman because they have mates at their side, who should want to build the proper foundation for a home as God has ordained it. It matters not how good the congregation looks upon a man and his works, if the home is in chaos-the church is in trouble. The time and energy that a man gives to the church, to the other females of the church, to the children and friends of the membership, should represent only a portion of quality family time.

"Love," says Shakespeare, "looks not with the eyes but with the mind." When love begins to reflect and re-evaluate what once was described as special and precious, the value tends to decrease because comparisons become the focus. A man cannot expect a woman, 50 years old to look and act like she is 25, because time has the ultimate decision. If the thought is that time has not been that kind to her-look a little closer at him. A man ought to recognize that the woman has aged and matured and so has he. He does not look 25 and even with bleach and glow – It's just not so!

"Real love does not act unseemly and is not puffed up," says the Apostle Paul. He admonished husbands to love their wives as themselves. If men love nice clothes, a clean home, well-behaved children, peace, good sex, security, good food, and affection, there ought to be a greater appreciation for the female of the family. A house divided cannot stand but God's word will draw the divisions and increase the blessings in order to manifest the prophecy. No man of God can fail to take care of home and family responsibilities and propose to take care of God's business.

When trouble is prevalent in the home, people tend to avoid going to church. Attending Church represents a visitation to a neighborhood theater where actors on a stage get up to play a part and then leave their role after dismissal to become the "real" person. It is sad when young children relate horror stories to teachers and others about the "behind closed doors expose's" that are similar to soap operas, and we laugh! Why? Because it reminds us of so many relationships. But oh, how sad, to personify this type of life on a regular basis without knowledge of the true and living God-a God, who seeks only good for our lives.

The most amazing thing of all is that everyone in the church knows everything about the situation, often long before some of the key players have a clue that they do. There will come a day when all of us will be glad to enjoy the mate provided for us. Short and tall, fat and skinny, pretty and not so pretty, educated and not so educated, dark or light complexioned, will not be a criteria for acceptance or denial-A day when we are so glad to be forgiven and given another opportunity to live together that we look for positives in all the wrong places and defy negatives to enter into any of the right places-A day when love looks beyond all faults, all failures and all hope to see precious meaning in all encounters.

For better and for worse is a privilege denied to so many and yet expected by those who marry for real love. What is real love? These days it's difficult to assess but you'll know it when you see it, understand it when you hear it, and feel like a millionaire when you suspect you have it!

This Song Is Dedicated to The One I Love!

Why is it so difficult for saved people to embrace the idea publicly of "love in the first degree?" Somehow we think that love songs like "Baby, I am for real," "What's love got to do with it?," "You are so beautiful," and "Baby, I love you" are sinful for Christians to hear. My question to the nay sayers is "what are the excuses that most men and women of the church use when they experience marital problems or divorce?" Check the records for yourself. Do research, if you will, on counseling issues that most pastors and other religious affiliation leaders encounter, then tell me what love has to do with it.

In retrospect, I look back over the years at my own marriage and go "oops," at the lost opportunity to share with hurting, young couples the fact that real love is not afraid to demonstrate. We do not discuss with couples the various kinds of love such as eros, phileo, stergo, and even the greatest of these–agape. As a matter of fact, we frown on those who enter the sanctuary holding hands, while gladly expressing a monogamous relationship. Most people are wonderful people, spiritual or secular, but we all have our own ideas when it comes to intimacy and its disclosures in the presence of parishioners. People see us enjoying each other throughout the week, however on our worship day–the mask comes on. The pious look of saintly privileges and "fleeing sin" overtake us. Our mate smiles in our direction and whispers "I love you," but we ignore them because the elders may be watching. How sad, when we forget that God is watching too. He must be grieving as we appear to ignore His Word. God told man not to allow anyone to put asunder the relationship He joined together. (I am paraphrasing, but it is the truth.)

Our hearts should be rejoicing because this thing, this feeling, this emotion, this earned revelation, is real. One song writer wrote, "Is it real what I feel?" Those of us who are seasoned in this matter know that it is. While marriages are breaking up or falling apart by default, some of us are sitting in the pews pretending. No one says, "go home and cut the lights down low, and, honor your wife or your husband." I believe that if leaders did this more often or at least one time, they would see their membership improve, increase, or at least have the tensions decrease.

Smiles and goodwill would abundantly reach out to the members, trust me, and the negative energy seen so frequently would give way to greater respect. Older individuals who have become bitter over the years may simply be frustrated and time allowed with a motivated, appreciated, well deserved mate, will create satisfaction and peace beyond belief. Even the leader may gain some thoughts from observing the transformation of those prayed for and renew his or her own vows. Be aware that the "amen corner" of the church probably won't tell you what I am sharing but sooner or later, somebody had better tell it like it is, or deal with the remnants.

There is a time for everything. Everything has a season and that means us and our relationships as well. (Ecclesiastes 3). What does that statement mean? Let me take my time to explain in my own way, my logic: Whenever you plant something, it has to grow and then be harvested but only according to nature's growth cycle. These are the laws of nature and the land. A child may be born today but will only walk, talk, and mature according to the stages of life's growth cycle.

Relationships have to follow a pattern of growth and development. You cannot cheat the system created by God or you pay a price of retribution. A church is a spiritual gestation period for the greatest harvest of all–the ascension of Christ.

"If it's real what you feel" for one another, no one can take the greatest moment of your life away from you. There is a light that shines from the depth of our souls when we see the mate given to us by God, enter our presence. It is difficult to resist the desire to laugh, to shout, to touch, to embrace, and to tell the members, after the sermon, "We have to go now. We will see you later. We have given God our best time of the day and now it is our time. We are the anointed of the Savior." Your mate may add, "I am leaving here today to be with my lady, my baby, my wife–who adds spice to my life. She is symbolic of the woman written of in Psalm 31 and my refuge when God has my requests on hold. She lights my fire and sparks my desire to go to work and pay the bills. She loves me like a rock and has insight like a fox. She is my massage parlor and my anchor in a safe harbor. She dresses like a queen and treats me like a king. When she steps out–my heart wants to shout with pride. This woman has my rib and we have learned how to forgive. She is fine and potent like fermented wine."

You may not see what I see, and that is as it should be. I see beyond the beauty, the weight, the disabilities, the age, the education, and the past–to the promise that love has made. Love is in the eyes of the beholder and I have a clear vision.

When It is all said and done and we finally get home, we pause and I hear him say to me "cut the lights down low–I have a love song for you and it is not in the hymnal. I want you to know when one of us departs this life before the other, that we have been truly blessed with a mate who loves as Christ loves the church and did not hesitate to submit to the greatest love on earth."

We only have one life to live, few second chances and few choices for wonderful mates, therefore, we have to nurture and continually improve upon the one we have. I feel sorry for those who don't understand or respect the power of true love because it is a tribute to God when we wait for guidance. If we are willing to recognize the voice of the Master leading and guiding us to a brighter future, there will be so many blessings bestowed upon us. Now, we will stop talking, "allow the mood, to develop, and let the music play our song."

Chapter 6

Poetic Reflections of Love & Realities of Life

A PARENT'S PRIDE AS NATURE SALUTES !

My darling children, I love you both–
Not because of the beauty you show,
And not because of the smiles you bring,
But for your intelligence wherever you go.

View the sun as it arises in the east,
For it symbolizes what makes us proud of you.
We are so proud as we watch your facial glow,
Like a blossom in the morning dew.

We welcome the moon on our darkest nights,
As we whisper thankful prayers of love.
Its shadow watches over each one of us
As a blessing shining from the heavens above.

Listen my children and you both shall hear,
Of the pleasing spirit that always abound–
In a house of love and parents so dear,
And the peace and joy that family is around.

EVERY DAY

Every day I look for miracles,
For blessings I did not earn,
Unmerited gifts to me, from heaven.
I know they are there because God promised them to me.
This wonderful Savior knows what's best for me,
And He searches my soul for the peace I seek.

Dark though the days, strange
Though the reasons, I see sunshine in the midst of the storm,
 Beckoning me to prosperity and health.
I have His assurance of a blessed tomorrow,
As He wills me to look ahead,
While telling me that I can make it!

SEE THE HANDWRITING ON THE WALL!

Look at your baby, our flesh and blood.
You deny her and refuse to acknowledge her presence,
But I can remember the time of conception.
I can remember the months of waiting,
And the pain–the excruciating pain of delivery.

I glimpse her fragile features so much like yours
And I clench my eyes so the tears won't escape.
I hear your promises of love forever in my ear,
And every physical memory tries to reappear.

How can you look at me and say there is no future
When every moment we shared was a life time in retrospect?
You request blood tests to prove you are not responsible,
And it hurts so badly because I have my pride.

I want you to remember as you press your claim
That my child will always have a name.
She will forever know that you are her father,
And despite your absence she was born with love.

She's mine, wrapped in humble naivete and care,
And though you've found happiness with someone else,
There are memories and events you cannot erase.
Don't look at "my" child through a court order attitude,
But remember that one day the story will unfold.

TAKE A LOOK AT YOURSELF

Nobody cares about my needs nor wants.
I struggle from day to day,
Trying hard to survive.
I tell myself that there is a way,
That the day will come when I will
Rise to inherit the benefits of life.
Some have never had to sacrifice,
To fail time and time again.
They have never had to dream big dreams
And have them fade into oblivion because of false interpretations.
Many have been hungry for truth and search endlessly,
For the peace that lives within.
They would rather sit on their laurels and reminisce,
Instead of holding to the truth of their heritage.

People care whether we live or die,
And those who believe it–express it,
With feeling of absolute proficiency.

But then I look around at others and I tell myself,
"Yes, someone will care."
Someone will remember the love and joy we
Shared and cling to good memories at my demise.
Yes, I must recognize that despite all of my problems
There are those who love me for me alone.
Did you look at yourself lately and find a special peace within?
Perhaps a mentor or a friend?
If so, you have found a secret pleasure which few can
distinguish for they think only
Of dollars and cents–But we know!
We know that the answer lies in taking
A look, not at others, but first at ourselves.

MY MOTHER

She used to stand straight and tall, grip the stairway railing and say, "One more time and I'll whip all of you until you won't think of sitting down again." Then she'd wait for a while–smile at each of us, and give us a snack of some sort.

THANK GOD FOR YOU, MAMA!

Hi Mama:

I know you are sitting up there and bending low,
To watch us celebrate your home-going row by row.
The choir is ready to sing and our friends are here.
Just to let you know that they loved you dear.

I was at church enjoying the service and song,
When the children came to say that you were gone.
I wept so hard because we never said goodbye,
Then I remember that with daily pain, you did reply.

So many things could have been different with you
But upon reflection, my life has issues too.
I hear folks now as they repeat things that you said,
And try to be nice about the life you led.

I miss you more than words can say
But I know that I must study and pray.

I can't forget the love, trials and care,
That I overcame because you were there.

You can rest now from the stress of this world,
For I will always be your little girl.
When you see Daddy, relatives, and my brother,
Tell them I've been born again and Jesus is my Savior.

Tell them that your love will encourage me,
And that's the reason I've learned to be free.
Rest now and be at peace,
When you get up we'll have a feast.

With all my love,

Your daughter

DEAR CHURCH SCHOOL MEMBER

_____(Date)_____

Dear _____(Name)_____:

I am so pleased to have you in my Sunday School class, as a church member and friend. When I think about the love of God and what He's done for us, I send up prayers for allowing you to be a part of my world.

We have come so far from where we've started from. Nobody ever told us that the road would be easy and that we would get tired of the troubles in this world. Trouble with family, friends and your neighbors, but we hold on because God is our source.

Every time you are ready to give up hope regarding some problem or situation, look beyond the cross to see hope, peace, love and joy. I cannot forget in my despair, to see Jesus hanging out on Golgotha's Hill, rejected by those whom he loved most. Who is _____(Name)_____ to feel the least of all upon remembrance of our Savior's death? He took the time out of his short life span to give us one more chance to accept His everlasting love. I will not allow anyone to make me doubt him because I know too much about Him.

He could have come down from the cross! He had all power in His hand. He could have chosen life over death but the world would not understand that Jesus is the author of life and death. He could have mocked the crowds and had the angels to knock His captives down, but instead He spoke forgiveness and gave His assurance that He has rooms reserved in His mansion for all who choose to come.

Some folks see the cross as the worst thing that can happen but I recognize that without the experience of the cross, I cannot reign with the Lord. There is no greater love at this season and every day of my life, than to know that Jesus died for me, _____(Name)_____. Your are a welcome addition to my class and our church in general.

Love Always,
Your Gospel Teacher

OUR POWER IS ALWAYS NIGH!

One day I got up from my bed and felt the need to pray.
I just wanted to thank God for one more day.

Joy came rushing to me while I was down on my knees,
And peace was hovering as a comfortable breeze.

I can't explain it, this miraculous birth within.
But the Savior knows who delivered me from my sins.

When I got to work there was a feeling of desolation
Which attacked my soul and I felt utter frustration.

The adversary was there to take my blessings of love,
to keep me from the success I had only dreamed of.

Something whispered so quietly within "peace be still."
Knowing that this too, is in the plan, is in the Master's will.

I couldn't understand, could not comprehend,
How these trials, these burdens, could be endured and I could be mended.

The adversary spoke and I cried with sad and grievous tears,
For I could not express my pain, my hurt, my fears.

I looked for my joy, my peace, my praise and they were gone.
It seemed that even God had taken a break from His throne.

At my moment of deepest despair, when there was not a friend anywhere...
I looked <u>up</u> instead of <u>down</u> and felt Jesus standing there.

He wiped my tears, calmed my fears and allowed me to be all I could be.
He met my adversary eye to eye and shook the chains that shackled me.

In a melodious voice He told the enemy to leave me alone,
For I was a chosen child, a praying child, that meant no wrong.

The adversary trembled and acknowledged this mighty Warrior,
Who had the power to tear down hatred, frustration and racial barriers.

I learned that alone, I cannot fight this evil power,
But God makes me strong like a mighty tower.

When I got home, I got on my knees in prayer once again,
Understanding now that without faith the adversary will win.

I know a Man from Galilee, and He's got a way with His word,
That allows your enemies to know that He's been heard.

Go to sleep, you can rest easy now for you have an advocate...
Who knows your heart and He's never, ever late!

One who knows your early rising to setting sun...
Who knows your life's work will soon be done.

DON'T LET THE WORLD FOOL YOU!

Look at the cool hour glass of time,
That look so peaceful, so sublime.
Yet if you falter– it is so revealing
As it continues its course while concealing
The many secrets that have not escaped
Searching hands and tears sometime faked.

Look at the streets so busy today.
Who knows the horror that travels this way?
The intersections are crowded with happy folk.
Many will tell you different but this is no hoax.
They were unidentified folk vibrant and alive,
Who traveled the same streets that we both drive.

Look at the sky with its beauty so grand,
Remember the planes that circle to land.
They replicate birds so high in the sky,
But when they crash many people die.
No matter the disaster–pain and fear,
Planes are boarded whether cloudy or clear.

Look at the people who seem so calm,
Who never think to run or sound an alarm.
If you turn your back and forget to be alert
You may be injured or subject to hurt.
Allow what you learn to become your tool,
And remember the elements will cause you to lose.

WHAT CAN I SAY?

I watched the police van leave the city–
As it transferred you and others to prison.
Tears ran down my cheeks as
I whispered, "what a waste!"
You were my life–my inspiration,
And now I am here and you are gone.

We both knew that this day would come,
For your way of living was day to day.
I prayed so often when you left the house,
And sighed with relief when you returned.
I sensed your restlessness as you paced the floor–
And saw your stress as the phone would ring.

I begged you to change your lifestyle,
But you only smiled and hugged me close.
And even though I saw through your daily lies,
I failed to believe what my eyes said was true.
You promised me the world and a two-dollar dream
But I knew the truth and your family did too.

All of us need you but you've become a number–
That obeys a system that chains and binds.
What can I say when the record is clear?
When will our love begin and this madness end?
I need your touch when my hours are lonely,
And there is no one else to fill the void.

The window pane is dark but I can see you.
I see your tears as the van moves on.
How many times must we go through this?
How many excuses will we continue to make?
You hold the key to your door of freedom,
Freedom to enjoy a peaceful and prosperous life.

The van continues on to its final destination
For it has an objective–a goal to reach,
But the two of us are not of the same mind-set.
We cannot go where the road does not lead.
I see you look up and our eyes say it all.
Your's say "don't forget about me"
But mine answer "what about me?"

MAMA, DO YOU HEAR ME?

What do I do when it hurts so bad?
Where do I go when I feel so sad?
Does anybody see beyond my smile–
That I've been abused and my body defiled?

It's a family secret that no one shares,
So nobody holds my hand or really cares.
Others say there is a problem with my mind
But don't understand the obvious signs.

I want to scream about this pain of incest,
But I've learned to conceal and not to confess.
My mama is in denial and my sibling's say I lie,
And pretend to others that I'm devious and sly.

Silently I reach for mama to take my arm,
But she ignores me for her "man's" charm.
I cry with despair and hold it within,
Knowing that my peace is not with my kin.

I must grow up to help abused children everywhere,
Though few may believe issues about their welfare.
I will be the one who will listen and defend,
The children who desperately need to mend.

If no one else will dare to take a stand–
On behalf of broken vessels all over this land,
There must be a me and a you out there,
To carry the "little" burdens we often bear.

FAMILY REUNION BLUES

Here we go again Family Reunion time–
Some seem wealthy and some without a dime
But we are all happy and that is our choice–
For coming together so that we can rejoice.

We've lost loved ones through death and grief,
We've had marital problems, permanent and brief.
Children and parents too have gone astray,
While families pray daily that they are okay.

Drugs and alcohol have invaded our homes,
Causing us to believe our hope is gone.
We've got babies born without love and guidance,
And young parents who deny it with strong defiance.

I admit that I have the family reunion blues
And you'll understand when you walk in my shoes.
I've got nothing great to brag about–
But I've got something I can shout about.

When I look back over My life to the past–
To the cotton fields, apple trees, and jimpson grass,
I count my blessings one by one
For I am grateful for what God has done.

When I think of my rundown shoes and cheap cotton suits,
I'm mighty glad that I know my roots.
When I think of family up yonder looking down,
I get joy because we'll meet on higher ground.

The family reunion blues is all over me,
Though I shake it off 'cause I want to be free.
B.B. King said, "Everybody want to know why I sing the Blues"
But we know that reunions are mighty good news.

Take the time to love someone while you can,
For all your efforts are in God's plan.
The enemy comes to find fault and to upset,
While the children of hope find little to regret.

Let's pray for our next reunion year,
For we don't know whether we'll all be here.
Family time is precious and quietly slips away,
That's why I told the blues it just can't stay.

PREACHER: ACCESS YOUR MEMBERS!

Preacher, I see wounded members in the pew,
Members, frail and weakened by the devil's brew.
A Member standing by the altar, tears on his face,
Aware that time has quickened its pace.

See the teenager acting out, wanting to be grown and on her own.
She has a baby on her hip and one to be born.
What are we teaching to prepare them for life?
They were made to have pleasure and then to be a wife.

Look preacher, at the deacons on the board–
Can you count on them when Christian morals are lowered?
Who lives a sanctified life among your people of the church,
And causes the sinners to reach for the Bible in their search?

What about your life and the Words you preach?
Do you live according to the commandments you teach?
How about family relationships and paying your bills?
Is your church growing people or busy making deals?

Reverends, Elders, Bishops, or Priests–whatever the name–
This observation is not meant to cause blame or shame.
It is an opportunity to assess our numerous situations–
Which effect members of multi-cultural church affiliations.

Sanctuaries are made up of people from all walks of life.
People who come to worship without malice and want to know Christ.
We refuse police checks and drug exams to identify potential thugs,
As we reach out, teach up, and smile while armed with spiritual hugs.

May I ask, "Brother–Preacher,
How about your members?"

WHO WINS IN THIS GAME OF LOVE?

What is Love when I'm often tossed aside?
What is love when my heart has been denied?
I've done all that I can to please and satisfy–
But all I've gotten is a sad good-bye.

You've risked all our hopes and dreams
On a one-night stand or so it seems.
What is love when I shed bitter tears
As you choose to forget our many years?

Children, home, and future don't matter much,
And needless to say–I won't be your crutch–
When the party is over and the pain begins,
And you want to come home in spite of your sins.

Who wins in this game of fast retreat?
Who will lose, me or your women in the street?
Keep in mind that I have goals to achieve–
With or without you, I plan to succeed.

WHO'S AFRAID OF YOU?

Fight, fight, fight is all I hear you say,
For fighting seems to be your only way.
There will come a day when I'm sure you'll find,
Yourself wishing, you were a friend of mine.
Just because you're smiling and feeling glad,
History will reveal that you aren't so bad.

You think you're hurting me but I am all right–
So keep on trying to win by starting a fight.
You instigate others to laugh at clothes I wear–
Telling all your friends that I refused your dare.
One of these days you'll be running your game,
And someone will stop and move you to shame.

I want an education so I can succeed.
You may be my client or a mouth that I must feed,
So fight if you must when you think you are right,
But choose your weapons with honesty and delight.
I suggest that you learn from the books that you see,
About living in an economic and human society.

You may want to take psychology for the living,
For If you plan to make it–you must be forgiving.
Keep on intimidating those you think are small,
And watch the future as it explains how to fall.
When you decide to fight you ought to do it right,
Take my advice and refuse this fight.

There is no reason to prove that you are the best,
That you have beat up a body wearing a dress.
As a matter of fact, I believe I can win,
But who cares when the dust settles–what then?
Everybody's got a dream of being strong with power,
Who knows? You may be "Who's Who of the Hour."

I WEEP FOR MY PEOPLE.

You what?

I WEEP FOR MY PEOPLE.

Why do you weep for me?
Am I not joyous, and
praising God in my own way?

I WEEP FOR MY PEOPLE.

There is no need to weep for me,
I am strong. Tomorrow I shall rise
to claim what is mine. I shall
drink and be merry. Marry and
divorce. This is my life.

I WEEP FOR MY PEOPLE.

Don't weep for me. Weep for yourself.
Weep for Mahatma Ghandi, Martin L.
King, and those who say they had a
Dream. They were the fools. Sitting
at lunch counters, fighting police dogs,
attacked at voting booths, and hated for the
Color of their skins. All for causes that
Remain the same. They didn't have to die.
Money and fame could have been theirs.
It would have showed them something,
Folks running around talking about pride.
Pride is when you have a joint by your side,
money in your pocket, and a weapon to speak for you.

OH, HOW I WEEP FOR MY PEOPLE.

Who are your people? Don't you know that an
Individual is nothing until he claims his fortune,
Until he recognizes that only the strong survives?
Weep for yourself because you dream while I
Actualize, you theorize while I analyze. You
Fight for hope while I teach men to cope. You stress
Religion while I mandate decisions. Don't weep
For me. Save your tears.

I WEEP FOR MY PEOPLE.

God answers: You are lost and cannot
Understand why I weep for my people. A
People who are lost to the ways of their Savior.
I weep not for myself, not even for you, but

for the youth who shall never really see
Tomorrow. I weep for the elderly who cannot
safely walk the streets of today. For the
parents who have given up their guardianship
In return for "love me now." I weep because
love stepped out on the wings of the morning,
And man jumped down to the brinks of darkness.
I can't understand man's logic, but I shall under-
stand it better when this life has completed its journey.
I hold the future in my hands. People
shall one day run to the mountains and say
"Hide me" and the mountains shall be removed.

Laugh at me, mock me, and criticize my name,
But watch the signs of the times. Watch me
Handing out miracles, one by one, and two by two.
And one day, when you shall need deliverance from
your follies and foolishness, I shall humbly proclaim
That you have made it through the storm.

WHY DO I WEEP? BECAUSE WE ARE OUR BROTHER'S KEEPER.
WEEPING CLEANSES THE SPIRIT.

A CHILD BORN TO DRUG ADDICTS CAN BE SAVED!

Who is that child so lonely and sad
Who mourns for both her mom and dad?
What happened to erase her smile so bright
That overshadows her joy and dulls her plight?

Perhaps if I ask sincerely and truly concerned,
She'll tell me what I've already confirmed.
As I approached, her eyes darkened with unshed tears.
While I merely attempt to lessen her fears.
"Can I help you?" Is there anything I can do?
No one will dare to hurt you.
Where are your parents at this time of night?
What can I do to make it all right?
Tears began to flow and would not stop
as I watched her little shoulders start to drop.

"They left me going to a house to buy crack
and though I've waited they haven't come back."
Everyday I get so scared that they will die
and won't come back to say good-bye.

We have no money, no food and no home
'Cause everyone knows we don't belong.
My parents: they lie, they cheat and steal
and nothing they do ever seems real.

The relatives throw us out and call us a name
for we are reminders of the addict's shame.
The children at school make fun of our clothes
but we have no choice in the life they chose.

I dream of a clean house, food and nice things
of this concept called parental love and what it brings.
I dream of a land with no crime and no drugs
where everyone cares and gives plenty of hugs.
I looked at the child, wise beyond her years
and suddenly my own eyes filled with tears.
I hugged her and promised to listen and be a friend
for I too, had been neglected and rejected by kin.

I'M NOT TIRED YET!

When I was young,
I was naive, untrained and unlearned...
Or so I thought!
Then I got to be a teen,
And I was a queen,
Ready for a ride to adulthood,
Looking good and energetic...
And I was right!
But then I was slowing down–
Enmeshed with life's many pressures,
And I was reminded that my youth was speeding
Down the highway of lost years and tears
And I am still alive,
And striving toward victory's call of middle age?
Old age?
Not me!
I'm ready for tomorrow,
Glad for yesterday,
But thankful for today,
For it is not promised...
So my message to you is...
I'm not going over the hill or looking for a special thrill,
But I am just glad this feeling is "Sho nough" real!

WHAT IS LIFE WITHOUT A FRIEND?

There is no friend anywhere like you
Who shares my problems like you do.
There's not a lily in this valley below
That provides the beauty that we both know.

There is something wonderful about a friend,
For they understand faults and failures within.
When you're sad and lonely they are there
Just to show you how much they care.

What is life all by itself with only family pride?
When you can reach across miles to a friend by your side.
You can never hurt a soul who is sincere,
For heartaches seem small when they are near.

I'm fortunate to have that special person in my life,
And it's helped me to be a better parent and wife.
When I'm down, my friend lifts me up,
And our joy fills life's empty cup.

TO WHAT DO I OWE THIS HONOR?

Don't call me brother and forget sister too
If what you say is not true…

Forgive me if I'm wrong but live and learn
and sometimes in life we begin to discern–
truth and lies and deceit and faithfulness
without the negative concept of hatefulness.

Tell me how you can break in my house and be my friend–
discount the years of love–how will it all end?
Tell me how the rules apply when you break and enter
and swear and plead that you do not remember.
How can you shoot, maim and kill without a cause
and never share sympathy or care to pause?

Perhaps you could help a soul in distress
who don't even know how they got in this mess.
Their only wrong was a companion to crime
and had no excuse but "The Signs of the Time."

You proudly boast of symbolic men like King
but your way of life doesn't mean a thing.
You sell dope to the already dysfunctional child
and then angrily protest about criminals running wild.

I'm concerned about your parents and their control
while many of your children lose their soul.
Even an animal recognizes and takes care of its own
Supports, respects and guides to a semblance of home.

Put something down and you've got it and gone
it appears that no one can leave you alone.
I call it as I see it – No felony – no misdemeanor
but disrespectful to people who deserve a winner.
You're dead set on making life operate by rules
despite the fact that you went to the best schools.
Your glass house is toppling day by day
with no hope beyond a physical display.

People paid a high price to open doors for you
in blood, sweat and tears so you could walk through
but you close each one with laughs and smart rebukes
and have the audacity to say "Put up your dukes."
Can't tell you nothing beause you know it all
though even Humpty Dumpty had a great fall.
Something had better wake you up to your life goals
Or you may be the one "For Whom the Bell Tolls."

WHO AM I?

In the days of slavery some called me a nigger!
Who was I?
In the civil War era they called me colored,
and I still searched for my identity.

In the late 50's I was Afro-American and/or Negro
Dashiki's and other strange African dress dominated our culture.
Then in the 1960's Martin Luther King, Jr. inspired the minority American the
    right to freedom of choice.

It was then that I heard a voice.
It called from a distance, compelling me to surrender,
> My fears – my tears
> My sorrow – for a bright tomorrow
> My indifference – for confidence
> My inferiority – for superiority.

But do you really want to know something?
I found that in spite of progress, still I had so specific identity.
It felt good, so much better to eat, sleep, pray, walk, talk, educate and
    be educated, almost where I chose,
But still I was not fully accepted. Something was lacking!

James Brown opened the door slightly with his hit recording, "I'm Black
    and I'm Proud."
A bursting pride seemed to explode throughout my very being.
The words held hope.
A fierce desire to obtain, to fulfill, to find peace and a certain
    understanding grew within me.

It was then that I, as an individual, became motivated.
I was now, not nigger, not colored, not African, but Black.
I was not Black per se but Black in spirit, in mind and in my
    struggles for human rights and humanity.

Blacks have always had a social class within a social class as I'm sure
    most cultures do.
But during a period when being Black was inferior and unacceptable
    to any race, you
seemed to go farther with a fair complexion, often called "yellow" or
    "mulatto" to be really counted. One other factor was long hair regardless
    of the skin pigmentation.

During those years, I kept wondering where I fit in.
I wasn't Dark Brown, High Yellow, or Black. I had drifted
Somewhere between dark brown and tan. Socially, I wanted
to be lighter but my choice of makeup destroyed that image.

All of you are the witnesses for my first announcement on
the pleasure I experienced when the Black personality, the Black
    pride era emerged.
It felt good to be myself! To be a poor, black girl raised
on welfare was all of a sudden, a stepping stone to a brighter future.

I began to seek educational endeavors which would guide me to a rewarding
    and more satisfying life. I want to retain the past so that when my children
    will one day want information regarding their heritage, I can say in
    response, "I've been there.
I had to climb some high mountains of servitude,
Cry some bitter tears of despair, but I made it and you can too."

"If the doors of opportunity still don't open, don't stop and give up hope.
Don't go on the streets or turn to dope.
Take a different direction and then say to America who's been proclaimed as
'The home of the brave and the land of the free,' to help you because
Your life as an American citizen is a testimony of survival and salvation."

I was truly blind to my identity but now I see an image.
I know who I am and where I'm going.
A few doors are open and I'm preparing to go through.
I've learned that until you recognize yourself and achieve pride in who you are and what you are, You remain nameless still asking the same question, "Who Am I?"

YOU CAN MAKE IT!

I was in trouble and my life in distress
God is my refuge when I've done my best
my strength when my friends disappear
my hope in times of fear.

My loved ones turned away from me
disappointments are not hidden from thee
I've been ready to give up on this lonely race
Jesus is waiting to wipe the tears from my face.

(CHORUS)

You can make it, you can make it

God gave me money, power and fame
and still I fail to honor His holy name.
Lord how frail, how impatient I've been,
I must confess that I've been truly blessed.

Oh, Lord – Count it all joy when you fall into temptation.
I've found peace in the crucified one–
knowing no enemy can triumph over my heart
for Jesus has claimed me for His own,
I must keep my mind and hold my tongue.

(CHORUS)

You can make it
You can make it
You can make it

Oh, Oh

You can make it
You can make it
You can make it

oh, oh

You can make it
I know you can make it
I know that you can make it.

I'VE ONLY GOT TO LOOK AROUND ME!

I don't need a doctor to calm my fears
I don't need a pail to hold my tears
I don't need a weapon for my neighbor
I don't have to prove that I've got a savior.

All I've got to do is look around me
And know that God has set me free.
He took my heavy burdens and loved me still,
He guided me and strengthened my will.

I don't need the assurance of a friend
To let me know, I have peace within.
I don't need the frown that comes on your face
When I've been saved by God's grace.
I'm so thankful for what He has done
For your presence and the Lord of God's son..
All I've got to do is look around
And I know my soul is heaven bound.

A LADY, BUT STILL MAMA'S BABY

Here you are a child again
Waiting for my nurturing to begin.
I hug you close the way I used to do
And whisper softly "I love you."

You're married, happy and aware
That besides your mate – my love is there.
When you were a child, we played –
And when you became an adult, I prayed.

Age will never erase our family ties
For kinship binds even though time flies.
So freely come to me and lie on my chest,
It is then that I know I've done my best!

KIMBERLY AND TARA: MY JEWELS

To both my daughters I love so much
   I give my daily loving touch
Your births meant the world to me,
   Surely all of this was meant <u>to be.</u>

Kimberly, my golden, vanilla baby was my first
   I was so proud – I thought I would burst!
Then came Tara, my loving chocolate baby
   Who loved to smile and seemed so lazy.

From babies to young ladies, I swelled with pride
   And taught them each how to tithe.
I taught them that education breeds success
   But it only comes when you've done your best.

I asked them not to count on man
   Or forget their goals without a plan.
And finally not to ever forget one another
   For that is a legacy from their mother.

Chapter 7

There is Humor In the Church As Well As Our Lives

I Stand Accused–But Am I Really Guilty?

    I would not be here today, but on Friday morning several members of our church invited me to attend a special program. They informed me that I would appreciate hearing such a distinguished and notable person as the guest speaker. I hurried home and put on my Sunday best dress, high platform shoes and dabbed a few drops of "Secret Sin" perfume behind my ears and I was ready.

    For protection on my walk to the church, I carried my Bible and a "five finger" soul Brother and Sister salute.

    When I arrived, everyone seemed to be quite excited about something. When the building was full, I was asked to come up front, and guess what " I was the special guest!" Shock was not the word. I was so proud. However, subconsciously I wondered what prize I had been singled out to receive. They lost no time in stating the purpose of the sociable if you can call it that! Those immature, hypocrites had the nerve to accuse me of transgression of three commandments on the holy book.

    Look at me, those of you who know me and judge fairly and justly. I am not perfect, but I must admire that although I stand accused, sometimes circumstances arise which are beyond our human control.

    Let me share with you their accusations and explain myself as best as I can. Can you imagine me dressed up liked a movie star on camera and getting disfellowshipped because of a few misdemeanors. My first crime was cited as being a thief. Several woman stood up and announced that they had seen me steal Sister Sally's husband from right under her nose. Well, this is inaccurate. I didn't steal him, he hijacked me on my way to the cleaners. I tried to warn Sister Sally to clean herself up. To stop wearing those odd clothes, and rummage sale rejects, to put on a little Baton Rouge and put a little starch on those limp wigs so they would stand out a hold out for a little bit longer. Her husband was so ugly, that I wouldn't have accepted him as a peace offering during World War Two. How could I steal something and I do mean "something" that grabbed and held on regardless of the "Assault and battery laws." You think about that!

    Then up jumps accusation number 2. Ms. Goody Two Shoes, my best friend or so I thought, accused me to my face (she couldn't wait till I turned my back) of murder in the first degree. When I asked her who I was supposed to have killed and when was the funeral scheduled, she laid it one thick. She accused me of "murdering with my tongue" Deacon Jones. Now let us examine the evidence on the square deacon. The offering was being counted on a Sunday morning. As I was going toward the background, I saw Deacon Jones slipped a few Tithe slips into his pocket. I stopped and mentioned it to him, the pastor, four or five other deacons, and any member who asked me. I couldn't tell a lie, could I? The pastor didn't take any action so I included him in my prayers for the unbelievers the next Sunday morning. My "friend"agreed with me on all counts and promised to support my campaign to withdraw all funds dating back to two or three years. Some of that money was mine! The pastor finally apologized and the Deacon stopped pocketing the money, I thought the incident was over. You think those two crimes of sin were sad, listen to the third.

My next door neighbor accused me of coveting her house. I was amazed! She said that everything they worked hard for and bought, I came over being nosy, and the next thing they knew, I owned it too. Her family bought a new car, and a few weeks later I drove a cadillac into my driveway. She bought Sears Original, and Sunday afternoon at the Tea Special we looked like twins. Somehow we even had babies a week apart. Can I help that? She accused me of being jealous because they make progress. I told her a thing or two before those folks. I told her to get her house in order because I was going to do a little house cleaning around our neighborhood after their crucifixion.

Now I have defined my problem and explained my concerns, I hope you can understand that I need to pray a little harder, keep my mouth shut until the proper season, and avoid temptation and neighbors as much as possible.

Please be careful when you talk, walk purchase material things and when you meet because you may be accused even if you are not guilty!

Thought: Seriously, though, life is a series of ups and downs. Most of all, it is reality – seeing a situation as it really is and facing it squarely regardless of the consequences.

I am sure that you have heard the expression, "Happiness is where you find it." My personal opinion is that it is an understatement. Finding happiness is not easy, until you learn that it comes from within but I urge all of you today to remember these statements on rumor and act accordingly.

1. Be cautious of someone who always has ill gossip about someone else's affairs.
2. Look for the best in others.
3. Be prepared for disappointments but don't always expect to be disappointed.
4. Honestly and sincerity is the key to a much happier life.
5. You will always stand accused in life, but don't be found guilty!

THANK YOU!

Ain't Church Funny...

Ain't church funny? Well, if it ain't, tell me why so many people keep laughing at the most inopportune times? And you know God is not pleased because we are in the sanctuary when the laughing starts. Church service is a sacred time and we should demonstrate quiet, loving and respectful behavior.

You know that I am right, so stop it. Don't do that anymore. I know you can't help it, but you are in church and I refuse to sit next to anyone who cannot practice self-control. Now where was I? Oh, I believe that whatever we see or hear in the church worship should never provoke laughter or broad grins on the faces of parishioners. We hurt feelings because people think we are laughing at them. We have to be conscious of our behavior and attitudes.

Can I at least share several incidents that describe funny things in church that many not have been funny to the individuals involved? Thank you for the affirmative because I am bursting to share the humor inside of me that is struggling for release. Keep in mind that I am a Christian.

Remember when the lady was singing and her underwear fell to the floor? Another time, a lady's skirt slid down while she was singing and she picked it up, put it back on and never missed a note. One woman's wig came off and she had small braids with different color rubber bands all over. Another time, a woman lost her wig during service as she praised God. Her husband, trying to be helpful, tried to put it back on but it was backwards. A group of singers came to town and as they sung out of their hearts, one of the member's false teeth fell out of his mouth. He picked them up, put them in his pocket and kept right on singing. I have to give him credit–he had a lot of courage and self-esteem.

Shouting, you know, emotionally praising God, can be so funny, although it should not be. One woman was drunk or high on some substance, came to church and put on a show. She brought her tambourine and tapped it to an off-key beat which drove everyone crazy. At the same time she did some rhythmic movements, also off-beat. Though annoyed, few people could keep a straight face. And don't forget the preacher that wore so many colors that he was dubbed the "NBC Peacock." Poor man, he was sharp. Check out the brother who came to church in all of his glory: a red suit, shoes, socks, hat, homemade sideburns and black hair-dye to match. He stood up proudly and often and all you saw was his finery as you tried not to focus on his outward appearance. I give him his props, the brother was cool and I am not player-hating, simply smiling as I share.

Of course, you had to see the woman who jumped up and did the "break down" dance at a high point in the service. And don't forget the person who shouted so strenuously that she ended up on top of several people and her feet stood straight up. Then there was the little child who was asked whether she wanted to be in the little children's choir. She said "yes" and the advisor asked her for her favorite song. She responded "Is it good to you" which was a R&B adult recording. The advisor expected to hear songs like "Jesus loves me" or "All the children of the world." Needless to say, the advisor didn't stop laughing after the child walked away.

We have to admit that Church is funny. We can't laugh in the sanctuary. That is not polite. Wait until you get at least one hundred feet from the church and (whisper) don't let everyone know why you are laughing because you never know who is related to who. You know people get so offended at the church.

Don't Fight the Heat Waves That Burn Inside of You!

I am sorry that I forgot to tell you about the changes that may occur as you get older. I suppose I should have said "will occur" but you never know about the modern day drug experiments with nature. Father Time and Mother Nature will talk to you soon enough. They will walk with you and send you signals that nobody will recognize at first but you.

Some of the signals are like smoke signals and others are like raindrops that keep falling on your head. Some resemble a burning bush that won't go out no matter what you do. These are times of revelation. They reveal more than you want to know about your life cycle. This brief reflection into the heat cycle as I know it is not meant to embarrass or shame but to elicit support and appreciation for what mature women endure in a gracious manner, I hope. Below I have listed some examples which I believe most women understand:

- When a seasoned and experienced woman of energy, who is vibrant and well defined enters this stage of her life, she must prepare for the ultimate–the heat wave, with flashes of heat, direct from the sun of her soul. Now she may assume that because there is a distinguished elder in the crowd, that she is not alone with these symptoms. Proceed with caution. If the woman were to look around, and see other seasoned women who are fanning rapidly with napkins, event literature, and the like; She would soon discover that not everyone, including the elder is not in the same mood with the elder in the crowd.
- If you can't get cool, no matter what you do, you are not in the throes of passion–you are having a "hot flash" commonly known as a characteristic of "menopause." This condition will increase or decrease depending on your stamina and physical state of health, or the herbs or prescribed medication you take.
- Women must know that this is not the Holy Spirit sending a divine message only to you when the wave begins to crest. Translated this simply means "Change is coming and preparation is not necessary, only acceptance." I believe in the Spirit of God but most of us who are seasoned get these same heated revelations. The divine revelation that the heat wave brings is not a mystery. Women in your presence will share their knowledge with a smile, a fan, a pat on the back, a hug, or a word of encouragement. The words may be "help this child Lord until her season is harvested. Have mercy until she passes through this wondrous period of her life. Give her strength to hold out or let the estrogen take over. You can do it Master, because you did it for me."

That Martha and those Vandella's had the start of this thing when they sang "It's like a heat wave, burning is inside me," but I am taking out of its context what I need to understand about my cycle of life. As a seasoned woman, you cannot buy this experience. You won't have a desire to possess it. You can't sell it or market it. You can't pass it on or pray it away. As a matter of fact, you can't give it away. Here are a few reasons why:

- At night, the covers come off abruptly and you use them to fan yourself. Your mate will initially be confused but will adapt given some level of negotiation for his comfort.
- There are also times when you fan your dress tail while you sit. Position is not a prerequisite for your "time of reckoning." When you feel its surge–it fills you. You will grab paper plates, magazines, anything to aid your discomfort.
- You may be the keynote speaker or the singing superstar but when the power of the heat wave comes, it brings its own band to play for you. It does not care about your title or who you represent–it has no problem with defining your degree of energy. There is no need to get too frustrated or annoyed because it has no boundaries. It moves when you move and retreats when you do otherwise it

does not have a hang-up when it comes to intruding on your privacy or greatest moment of public victory.

My husband once told me not to touch our thermometer as I rose to adjust the temperature during one of my crises. "Don't touch that thermometer," he said. "You can't regulate yourself. Everyone else is fine. You are having a flashback." After I thought about what he had said for a few moments and gave him my profound intellectual look, I responded. "I am having hot flashes. If I were having flashbacks in anyway, shape or form, you brother, would be in serious trouble."

There are many humorous incidents regarding this dilemma with hot flashes and I cannot tell them all. However, one friend does cause me to smile when I see her in church with her battery-operated fan in one hand and a manual one in the other. I am the third option to provide fan service when she is having a stressful day with heat and perspiration. She has a severe physical ailment which induces the warmth and my heart goes out to her. When I see her fans come out, I smile and we understand. She will whisper "girl, it's bad today" and then we laugh softly so that we don't disturb other parishioners. Sometimes we have a fan waiting for whoever gets to church first so an usher won't have to bring us one. One thing we know for sure is that we will get one from somewhere before the service is over.

Oh well, if it's not one thing–it's another. Your time will come, sooner or later. I hope it will be later so that you can enjoy your hot summer days and cool winter nights without a fight over the temperature in the house. Let this be a guide to the heat wave experience and don't be surprised when the day comes and you can't get comfortable. Take some advice from those who have been there and done that and live to the fullest.

WHAT HAPPENED TO US?
WHEN DID WE GET OLD?

Look at us sitting here like old folk
Both of us trying to figure out who last spoke.
You used to thrill me and now you threaten to kill me–
I used to hold you and do the things you told me.

Look at us sitting here growing old together
Forgetting that it takes both of us to make it better.
I find myself asking "What is a kiss?"
What in this relationship am I starting to miss?

The only time we get "real" excited is watching TV
And now it doesn't matter what we see.
Neither one of us rushes to open the door
And my nights are sleepless while you snore.

Romance will be greater they say, with age–
But if this is a sample, I'm becoming afraid.
I've been your woman and you've been my man
For so long that we've forgotten to plan.
This life we live is a one-way trip,
And it's important that we stop and get a grip–
Of what's happening in our golden years,
That block our progress and increase our fears.

You belong to me and I belong to you,
And we share a love meant for two.
Take a look at us–we are not too old for fun,
Let's remember how to hug in the sun.

Chapter 8

Life's Many Messages to Comfort & Guide Us Professionally

A Healthcare Professional On a Mission of Integrity & Faith!

No one is indispensable but you ought to be visible enough in your role that when you are absent–you are missed. People ought to know who you are, recognize you by your professionalism, and the quality of service you provide. A smile to the homeless as well as the elite must be your trademark. Above all, a pleasant personality is your best calling card.

When a job has been successfully completed, you are the example of respect and appreciation. Be the first to send a card, shake a hand or extend a compliment and congratulations. Jealousy and envy cannot be a part of your vocabulary because you know where your blessings originate. You are the one who must make things happen for others and God will make things happen for you. As health care professionals, in whatever capacity you play–excellence and integrity must be your guide. None of us asked for our culture, our race, our ethnicity, our gender and other differences. It will be up to us determine what to do with whom we become.

When trials come to defeat us and destroy our dreams, we have to reach beyond the circumstances in order to pull from our inner faith for strength. It is easy to accept an opinion given to us and give up but those who have been knocked down time and time again, know how to get up, look up, reach up, stand up, stay up and pray up. Sometimes your world is rocked from side to side with no notice to prepare you for coming events. Many times there is nothing and no one to hold on to. Your strength, ever present, reminds you to read the Word of God for consolation for you are standing on sinking sand. Hope is ignited and like a fire it spreads throughout your spirit. You are able to encourage others who thought you were defeated.

The storm that you assumed would sweep you away has been stilled and all is calm. You learn that your degrees, your titles, your job, your knowledge, your colleagues, your loved ones, cannot prevent trouble from knocking at your door. Your defense, my friends, is in arming yourself with faith and agape love. This will help you meet the challenges that will come. If you have been fortunate in this life and have not encountered any of the misfortunes I have mentioned, feel blessed but as sure as you live trials will come. When they do and you find that you are unprepared, remember that there is a Word for those who believe and live by faith.

I've had to walk with pain, bear the blame, and hear my name used in vain, but I know how to hold up my head and let love sustain the body that is my frame. I understand how trouble and sorrow will creep in unannounced and many of you do as well. We provide services and we utilize the services. As we suffer, we recognize the symptoms in others and remember that they are not statistics, they are human beings who like us, deserve to be nurtured. You, the blessed, the anointed, the trusted, the suspected, the respected and often neglected–you create an atmosphere of mercy and compassion in some of the worst situations and often for the worst of individuals. Those of you who wear the label, African American and some labels given to you that I will not mention, reach out to those who do not have adequite care, those who dare you to help them, and some who don't have a clue regarding their needs. You are the difference. The difference beyond expectation, beyond the procedures and rules, beyond the code of your premier schools--you are the vehicle, the fuel which motivate the self-proclaimed world class organizations to succeed. You are the glue that brings communities together. If preventative medicine, wellness and healing will produce improved health care systems, then you must be the winning trend setters who must operate within and without for success among your people and your customers.

Hold up your hand, give a high-five to someone next to you and repeat after me: "I do my best every day. I give my best from day to day. I try not to second guess as I plan my day. I look for the best in those I serve. When I give my best, and feel less stress–I know that I am blessed. Thank you!

People Perish for Lack of Knowledge and Commitment...

You bet I am mad. I am so mad that I want to live. I want to live so that I will make a difference for somebody. They may not like me–may even hate the message that I bring but that is all right because I know who I am and I know who my source is. I know the One who has my best interest at heart. He is the One who directs my thoughts as I share them with you. May I speak from the heart to African-American women who are dying of breast cancer and other chronic diseases at a faster rate than any other race? May I speak in a vernacular which will be understood, if not appreciated? Now is the time to tell the truth or be the truth, and I refuse to leave this moment without a voice, crying in the wilderness of our despair.

"Sophisticated folks don't want you to mention God because we got to be careful who we offend, but I am so darned confused. When the children in school–you can't talk religion. But when they out of control and the system can't make them mind–they call for anybody's gospel. They will make them children take a Bible. I am so confused. Folks come to us giving away help to the needy and the needy won't come get it. Take breast cancer, for example: The Surgeon General announced, "black folk are dying at a faster rate than any other race"–get your breast checked–it may save your life. I listened because I lost too many friends and relatives to the disease. I went right down there and was pulling my top off before they knew what I was doing.

I don't play with God's property. I told some of my friends to go for a check up too and they said, "I ain't messing with my breasts–they ain't bothered me this long and I'm leaving well-enough alone. If you start messing with them–they bound to find something wrong. Girl, don't you let folks fool you. There ain't no epidemic. Everybody gets sick, sooner or later. I thought you had some education, at least more than I got."

And so we continue to die because of superstition and lack of knowledge. I am so confused because I want us to live and be whole and healthy. Folks, from heaven knows where, may be giving away cheese and peanut butter, and we go miles to get it and don't really know where it comes from. What kind of logic is that? I see hurting people, ill and impoverished, without insurance and a lack of hope but who deny or ignore a fatal disease. Who is in need of a physician?

Now, if you want to upset me, let me see a woman putting another woman down because she's got it going on. You know, she got a decent man, a nice home, a few dollars in the bank, and they know how to put a smile on their face. They seem to work together and if they fight, they do it behind closed doors and then they come out looking like they done "found a love." I tell anybody, don't ya'll knock it, if you never tried it.

Some people in this world are crazy and I don't understand why, unless I got a few loose brain cells as well. But can anybody tell me why doctors got pills to make you high, to bring you down, to make you normal (so they say), and to work on your nerves–but nothing to help you explain to people how to live healthy, with common sense.

Listen, they even got pills and things to help with that romance moment. You heard about the pills advertised on the tv and radio? Folks been trying to write their own prescriptions and getting into all kinds of trouble. Doctors can make anything–so don't laugh at them when they talk about something you never heard of before. They can make a baby from only God knows whose sperm in a tube, make a woman into a man and likewise, but they can't make folks do what they need to do to help themselves. I told you that this is a strange world. We could improve human relations in this world if folks would come together and support each other. This is a journey that cannot be walked alone. It takes one making a difference for the other one. I may not make it to health and prosperity but it won't be a result of my neglect, or avoidance–it just may be my time to move to another level.

I am still mad but also glad because I have this opportunity to talk with you. I am glad to be here because I was invited and to be invited means that they want you to be there, or they got too many tickets, or they are afraid of somebody and you ain't–or they are broke and you've got extra. Whatever the reason, I'm glad to be here 'cause everybody knows that I'm a home girl. I believe in telling it like it is or is it "ought to be?" I don't know what will help the situation but if I say it and I am not asked to leave, I guess they accept it. Out of all we have been through, ain't it a good day–just like we were blessed on yesterday!

Survival Is Life's Make-over for the Soul!

Breast cancer is so invasive to a majority of women and also men that conferences are being held throughout America to educate women in particular, regarding this life-threatening illness. I was asked to be the keynote speaker at one major breast cancer event. Here is the context of my speech:

Good evening, my sisters and brothers. All praises and thanks to the Master of the universe who is the giver of all perfect gifts. Honor to the Mayor and city officials, ministers, physicians, health care representatives, community activists, and last, but the greatest, among us are the breast cancer survivors and family supporters.

We are here tonight to invite, excite, ignite, and certainly to rewrite your prescription for survivor. One day you experienced a "Midnight" in your life. Some of you cried and some of you denied the symptoms and ignored the lumps. Some of you felt hurt and discouraged as you waited with bated breath for the doctor to explain. Others questioned their faith and God with anger, "why me, at this moment, this time, this juncture of my life. Why now, when I have so much to live for–to say, and to do?" When surgery was over, some individuals looked over at their mate, their lover and friend, and said, as they pulled off their clothing, "Don't look at me. Remember me as I looked before: Healthy and whole. Remember my beautiful hair, the energy in my talk and the strut in my walk. Don't remind me of what I used to look like. Remind me of who I am today. A woman that you know intimately and spiritually. A woman who came from a "midnight" experience and discovered her "highlights." A woman who still thinks and reacts with divine order, understanding and balancing the endless change which has invaded her physical person. A woman who represents change that develops when we are least prepared and often not aware.

A woman is in a constant flow of energy, renewed and reviewed by all who care to know her. She smiles because she appreciates each morning that the sun rose for it is a sign that tells the world that she "woke up with her mind stayed on her Savior." There is a song in her heart that has a sweet melody which whispers, "There is a bright side somewhere. Don't you stop until you find it. There's a bright side somewhere." Late at night, when the evening and loneliness come, I can hear her sing softly, "This little light of mine, I'm going to let it shine. Jesus gave it to me and I'm going to let it shine." What you must not forget is that as you go through this storm of health and uncertainty in your life is that God is with you. You will learn to sing and pray even if you are not a believer.

Of course, you could possibly survive with the blues or maybe you could moan with rhythm and see how good you feel. One song in particular: "Why am I treated so bad? Why am I treated so bad? I'm all alone singing my song–hear my cry, although I've done nobody wrong–Still I'm treated so bad." After you sing that song a few times, you may be feeling fine but everyone around you will have all of your earlier symptoms. Whatever you are going through in your lives–know that you have life. A life that is vibrant, sacred and filled with the blessed assurance of Savior's love. You are never alone. Never forsaken. Never desolate. Never dead to your dreams and hopes for the future. Never defeated. You have the power of the resurrected Christ to take you through whatever may come against you. In the mighty name of Jesus, you can be delivered.

Sin did not place this disease in your body. Shame will not remove it. Denial will not erase it and grief will not ease the disappointment. Love is the only answer. To help save others, we must be honest and reach out to them with our message of life, deliverance and hope for the future. My sisters, we are all survivors of one circumstance or another. Let me leave you with some survival techniques regarding the make over of your soul:

1. Take care of you and your needs. You don't have to apologize for being selfish because few people understand what you've endured physically and emotionally.

2. Stay motivated in your goals and try new things, make new friends, and greet each new day with a new attitude.

3. Take a vacation and if all else fails, go next door to a friend's house, if you rarely visit, and please enjoy the time away. Positive relationships make a difference when you need to be comforted.

4. Rest in the physical and mental part of your refreshed spirit by reading the Word of God, sleeping, praying, and by being still while you meditate on the promises made and blessings designed just for you.

5. Let go of the many stresses that hinder your peace of mind. After all, God did not bring you this far to leave you. You can freely release your guilt by saying "no, no, no." Well, maybe you can say "yes" if it's your mate and the hug is just right.

6. Don't alienate your friends and those who love you. Support means a lot to you and to them.

Above all that you do, remember that you are an anointed child of the King. There is nothing that you cannot ask of the Father and he will not do for you. Hold fast to all of your hopes and dreams for you are still in the race.

You Are Not Defeated – Stand Up & Accept Your Success!

We are not defeated! We do not have to apologize to anyone for our struggles, our challenges, our joys, our misfortunes and even our failures coming up through the years.

Now is the time for us to realize that we are undefeated. That we can stand up and accept our success. For years we have been told to cook, to sew, to clean our homes so that we could be good wives. Then, we got the <u>real</u> scoop! Now not only will you clean, sew, and cook, but you can work full time, manage from two to "umpteen" children, and be a great lover. I know most of you feel very fortunate with those liberated statements and are desperately trying to discover what sociology, human relations, or psychology programs I read during college to surmise thoughts about your life-styles.

These statements apply to some of us and others will not relate. We live in a society which perpetrates myths regarding our role as a woman. When we accept those myths, we are encouraged to accept a set of half-truths.

Some myths we have to constantly combat are: (1) The U.S. is a country devoted to the preservation of the family. Women, after divorce, live a life of idleness maintained by alimony and child support awards. In actuality, more sympathy and favorable treatment is given to male-headed families in contrast to a female-head of the households. Women face prejudice from a male dominated society for being divorced. Times are changing but speculation has not. (2) Women do not work in the home. Etc...

As religious believers we must stand for something or we will fall for nothing. You may belong to any denomination but unless you have the love of God within, regardless of the recipient, you fail to please the believers or yourself. The truly happy individual is the one who looks back over faults and failures and recognizes that without the strength and power from a higher source there would be no victory. Some of us foolishly say "you see this kingdom? I did it all by myself and when I leave this world I'm taking it with me." And the world says "Go right on man. Oh tell me how!"

As employees and employers, we must be the first to do what is right for all concerned. Honesty and courtesy begins at the top and filters down. You can't promote what you don't accept. You can't give out what you don't have in. In most of our jobs we are dominated by males, but males don't have to dominate us.

We can only be put down by submission. We can only be torn down by allowing others to dictate our positive mind sets and losing our self-respect. Refuse to be isolated because you find peace in solitude. Refuse to be lower paid because you never stop seeking for the appropriate methods of resource development. Look for success in the smallest assignment. Think team and play whatever position you are asking for one day when the game is over, and the coaches are looking for a new team "who knows, you may be up to bat." And if the home runs keep coming, you may rarely have to play outfield.

You are not defeated–you've come a long ways from where you started from. All you've got to do is remain firm in your beliefs and faith. Wherever you are and whatever you are doing, stand tall and accept your success.

As a wife, we must be a friend and lover. Perhaps even at times, a sister to a brother, but that's okay because we set the ground rules for our homes. We become supporters for our mates and peacemakers when the battle hymn of the republic is echoed in our relationships.

As parents we have to play, and speak, and stay, and teach, and preach, and cry and refuse to deny our rights to challenge any and all decisions, and love, and love, and continue to love. We have to tell our children that the rock the dope pushers are selling will only last for a few moments but the "solid rock" on which the individual may stand is the foundation of life and all other ground is sinking sand. We must teach our sons and daughters that there is no need for abortion when we first initiate prevention.

As educators, we must tell the at-risk, the nontraditional, the negative, and the proud, that they can learn, and will learn because the opportunities are there for success to occur. Why can I say that with assurance? Because success comes with planning and planning with philosophy, a premise of "I can," "I expect," "I won't reject," "I accept," "I teach by precept and concept, and the goal is always to project." When I know that I know what I know, it is easier to live by the principle of self-actualization.

As a community leader, I must live in my environment, secure and safe in the knowledge that my family is protected, but aware that everyone else is not so fortunate. I must keep in my consciousness that "I am my brother's keeper." I must remind myself when I become critical and judgmental of the circumstances of my neighbors, that except for the "grace of God, there go I." And if I don't plan to help, I ought to be quiet and honor those who do.

Life Is Like a Kitchen Singing the Diversity Blues!

Sometimes my life has personified kitchen appliances and these are but a few examples: <u>I'm called a refrigerator,</u> my temperature is regulated by the power of energy. I am calm, cool and collected, with a variety of choices and selections but available only to those who choose to open the door.

<u>Sometimes I'm a freezer,</u> frozen for self-defense, because to show too much emotion or to give consistently with little return, is to unthaw rapidly, causing others to spoil, personal suffering and a lack of gratitude in return.

<u>I'm like a dishwasher,</u> going through life's cycles of change and unrest. My tears are refreshing and though they reflect my spirit of unhappiness, I must also, concede that they are often of joy. I release my force based on instructions provided and I complete the process according to the load I bear.

<u>I imitate a table</u> because my arms are wide spread to receive the blessed assurance of all who desire love, peace, and truth. One day a table was prepared for me, even in the presence of enemies, therefore I have no need of apologies. I don't have the audacity to remove anyone from the food of life and the bread of my salvation? "Oh taste and see," I recommend to all who doubt that my table is spread.

<u>See me as a stove</u> because my flame comes from within and no man can extinguish my glow. I have been cooked thoroughly but I am described as tender. I am a fire starter who sits alone but, draws a crowd because a "spark" of truth and creativity will ignite an entire area if your motive is real.

And finally, believe that <u>I'm like the counter top</u> because all the food preparation begins and ends with me. I don't have to worry about whether or not the refrigerator, the freezer, the dishwasher, the table or the stove gets the credit because none of us can work alone without some assistance from one of us. We respect each other and know our roles. The truth of the matter is that without the plugs, the handles, the legs and the resources, I am nothing but a fixture in a room. I am a testimony of all who question my cultural abilities and emotions. I represent diversity in the highest form. Not just for nepotism, or favoritism, but humanism. I am a kitchen aid miracle of discovery for I am user-friendly and my testimony knows how to sing the blues. Plug me up to your team-building concept and, regardless of our differences, and varied roles, we get the job done or get repaired.

You Can Play on God's Team if You Know Your Position

If you are willing to listen to God speak to you, you can have what you say. God has a great team called believers. Believers were selected according to their faith to be on the team. Tryouts are held for literal teams for exceptional talent and speed.

Great men and women of God played great roles on the gospel fields and received blessings for their labor. The desires of our hearts are only a prayer away. God loves us enough to do anything but fail. He wants us to have the best, for He knows what we have been through to get this moment.

You cannot play unless you are willing to think "we" instead of "me." You cannot play if you are unwilling to practice what you teach.

You must have a testimony on the power of God. What he did for you must be told or the world will never know Christ in the truest sense of the world. Don't limit his blessings to you, for he wants you on the team. He wants your physical presence. He could use anyone but he chose you. Won't you look for an opportunity to join the team? Don't wait for an invitation. Call Him up, through prayer and supplication, and He will come.

You can only play with the right attitude, love for man-kind and a sincere and prayerful life. But you *can* play because those who are annointed play to win.

Bertha Carson-King
appreciates your purchase of her book
"I Am Who I Am... A Work in Progress."

If you are interested in purchasing a larger quantity of books, hearing her powerful and anointed testimony, or her thought-provoking presentations on a variety of topics, contact the author at:

Bertha Carson-King
Car-King & Associates
P.O. Box 8689
Benton Harbor, MI 49022

or you can call:
616-926-4344